Momentum In Ministry

Momentum In Ministry

A DRIVING FORCE BEHIND THE CHURCH

JAMES SMITH
AND
DAVID CHURCH

MOMENTUM IN MINISTRY

Copyright ©2010 PreachIt Inc. All rights reserved.

No part of this book may be printed or reproduced in any manner whatsoever without written permission except in the case of brief quotations embodied in critical articles and reviews.

ISBN: 978-0-9828140-1-7

PreachIt Inc.
234 W. 166 S.
Valparaiso, IN 46385

Book Design www.KarrieRoss.com

Acknowledgments

There is no one I would have wanted to co-author Momentum In Ministry with aside from David Church. His knowledge of the scripture is extraordinary. He also knows full well the wrestling that nearly every pastor understands concerning the concept of building and the dangers of losing momentum in the local church. The church Dave pastors exemplifies this struggle for momentum and is one where there is a constant push towards increase, growth and maturity. The intensity of Dave's desire to be a blessing to other people's ministries was a driving force behind the completion of this book. Thank you Dave, for your willingness to be used, to cause momentum in the ministries of men and women, all around the world.

I also want to say how much I appreciate my wonderful wife. I write these words on the eve of our 25th wedding anniversary. You've made these the best 25 years of my life. You've been an incredible blessing to me and my ministry and you have always encouraged my writing. Thank you! Kristi and Jeremy, you are the best daughter and son a father could have.

James Smith

Acknowledgments

It has been a privilege and honor to minister alongside Jim Smith for almost fifteen years now. Jim is not only a fellow minister, but has become one of my closest friends. One of the things that Jim is very passionate about is helping and encouraging the ministry. I have been a firsthand witness of his passion for many years. His expertise in ministry brings a practicality that always transfers into results. Jim first shared his passion about this book with me a little over a year ago, and over the course of the last year we have partnered together to share with you a practical application of Momentum in Ministry. Without his passion for ministry, this book would not have been possible. Thanks Jim, and keep the momentum going.

I would also like to thank my precious wife Holly, my wonderful children, Adriene, Davis and Barrett. Their support is immeasurable.

David Church

Dedication

We dedicate this book to the thousands of men and women like ourselves who have struggled to raise up a church for the glory of God. Your sacrifice and labor is not in vain. God sees where you are at right now. We pray that what we share with you here will encourage your labors and give you a few more tools that you will need as we labor together with Him.

CONTENTS

Preface 13

Introduction 15

CHAPTER ONE:
What is Momentum? 23

CHAPTER TWO:
God's Nature 37

CHAPTER THREE:
God will have a People 43

CHAPTER FOUR:
Creating Momentum 59

CHAPTER FIVE:
Maintaining Momentum 75

CHAPTER SIX:
When the Enemy Stops your Momentum 89

CHAPTER SEVEN:
How timing affects Momentum 95

CHAPTER EIGHT:
Building Momentum for the Altar Service 111

CHAPTER NINE:
Momentum in Leadership 125

CHAPTER TEN:
Momentum Balance 141

CHAPTER ELEVEN:
Momentum in Preaching 147

CHAPTER TWELVE:
Team Effort and Old Paths 157

CHAPTER THIRTEEN:
Setting People Up For Success 171

Preface

Have you ever tried to stop a train? Of course not! A person would be foolish to try.

If you've ever noticed a long freight train, some of the engine cars face forward and others face the back. Interestingly, the engines facing the back are not used to move the train forward. Although they are in constant motion, they are only used if the train needs to stop. They are the brakes.

The average freight locomotive weighs 14,000 tons. With over 100 cars moving at a speed of 55 mph, the train is unable to stop on a dime. In fact, it takes that train— with all of its reverse engines and hydraulic brakes activated—over one mile of track to stop in the best of conditions. Why? Because momentum is at work.

Many people have perilously tried to race across railroad crossings in an attempt to beat the train, only to meet with disaster. Mistakenly, they think the engineer can simply reduce speed enough to give them ample time to cross. But every engineer knows that not only is it extremely difficult to stop the train's momentum, it is also very dangerous.

Attempts to stop a large train too quickly on a curve will cause it to derail, causing even more loss of property and life. The derailment often occurs when the momentum of the rear cars surpasses the momentum of the front ones. As a result, the cars in front are pushed off the tracks.

Few things demonstrate momentum quite like a moving freight train; its incredible mass and power continue long after the application of its accelerating force. Few things, that is, except God's Church.

No force on Earth is greater than the God of creation and no load larger than the souls of mankind. So great was this weight that Jesus Himself was the only One able to bear the burden of sin.

The momentum that started at Calvary has been building for thousands of years. The load, too, has grown heavier with each passing year. Mankind is nearing 7 billion people. No generation before has experienced the weight of humanity as much as ours has. God is causing the momentum of His Church to grow in every city and village of every continent.

Momentum is building. Speed is increasing. The Church is expanding. Revival, like never seen before, is just around the bend.

Habakkuk 1:5:

> *"Behold ye among the heathen, and regard, and wonder marvelously: for I will work a work in your days which ye will not believe, though it be told you."*

MOMENTUM IN MINISTRY
INTRODUCTION

The Parable of the Talents

Matthew 25:14-30

14 For the kingdom of heaven is as a man travelling into a far country, who called his own servants, and delivered unto them his goods.

15 And unto one he gave five talents, to another two, and to another one; to every man according to his several ability; and straightway took his journey.

16 Then he that had received the five talents went and traded with the same, and made them other five talents.

17 And likewise he that had received two, he also gained other two.

18 But he that had received one went and digged in the earth, and hid his lord's money.

19 After a long time the lord of those servants cometh, and reckoneth with them.

20 And so he that had received five talents came and brought other five talents, saying, Lord, thou deliveredst unto me five talents: behold, I have gained beside them five talents more.

21 His lord said unto him, Well done, thou good and faithful servant: thou hast been faithful over a few things,

I will make thee ruler over many things: enter thou into the joy of thy lord.

22 He also that had received two talents came and said, Lord, thou deliveredst unto me two talents: behold, I have gained two other talents beside them.

23 His lord said unto him, Well done, good and faithful servant; thou hast been faithful over a few things, I will make thee ruler over many things: enter thou into the joy of thy lord.

24 Then he which had received the one talent came and said, Lord, I knew thee that thou art an hard man, reaping where thou hast not sown, and gathering where thou hast not strawed:

25 And I was afraid, and went and hid thy talent in the earth: lo, there thou hast that is thine.

26 His lord answered and said unto him, Thou wicked and slothful servant, thou knewest that I reap where I sowed not, and gather where I have not strawed:

27 Thou oughtest therefore to have put my money to the exchangers, and then at my coming I should have received mine own with usury.

28 Take therefore the talent from him, and give it unto him which hath ten talents.

29 For unto every one that hath shall be given, and he shall have abundance: but from him that hath not shall be taken away even that which he hath.

30 And cast ye the unprofitable servant into outer darkness: there shall be weeping and gnashing of teeth.

Jim's Comments:

Fourteen years ago I began a career as an investment advisor. After spending weeks studying for the state and federal securities exams, I began a very successful, though brief, career. Successful, because I was landing sales of which most security brokers only dream.

After spending years as a house painter, I felt that I had found my calling. I loved the idea of helping people find ways to invest their money to achieve the greatest amount of profit for the least amount of investment risk. The idea of making money *with* money thrilled me. Imagine, making money not only during the 9-to-5 work day, but also making money while asleep.

After only a few months in my new career, I attended a securities symposium in Indianapolis, Indiana. For a full week, investment firms presented their funds, boasting their returns as far back as 20 years. For several days, I sat through presentation after presentation from some of the largest and most prominent investment firms in the world.

With Power Point presentations, each firm showed annual returns that all seemed to point upward when it came to opportunities for investment. With a room full of some of the most successful sales advisors, these firms worked to convince us that their funds were the best investment for our clients.

By the time I headed home from the symposium, my head spun with excitement. I knew that some of these investments were exactly what many of my clients wanted and needed. That night I went to bed still excited about what I learned and the potential to help my clients increase their savings.

After I slept several hours, a loud booming voice awakened me saying, **"The kingdom of God is the best investment!"** The voice frightened me. I looked over at my wife, expecting her to be fully awake and as startled as I was. But she was sound asleep. "Did you hear that?" I said, nudging her awake. "Hear what?" she mumbled. I realized it was the voice of God, reminding me that His kingdom was the best place to invest. It pays the highest dividends and interest and, best of all, there are no penalties or risks of investment loss.

I had just assumed a pastorate of a small struggling church, and I believed that God was telling me to leave my new career as an investment advisor to pastor the church. As a result, I turned over my clients to another advisor and resigned my position. But I never forgot my love of investing or the voice that reminded me that the kingdom of God is the best investment.

My burden to write this book comes from Matthew 25:14-30. This passage is a reference for us to follow for investing in people-resources. Although this verse holds many interpretations, I believe this passage is God's mandate to the ministry to invest our resources wisely for the sake of the Kingdom.

When I was in the securities business, it was my job to help my clients find that special fund or set of funds that were best suited to their investment needs and desires. If my client profited from the investment I suggested, they would sing my praises and recommend me to their friends and family. If, however, they lost money or— in the worst scenario— lost all their money, they blamed me, not the companies who invested poorly. After all, I was their financial advisor who made the recommendations.

Introduction

I know full well the burden and responsibility of investing wisely—especially other people's money. The above scripture illustrates how the Lord is an ardent taskmaster who punishes those who invest His resources poorly, but rewards those who use His resources wisely.

Nearly seven years ago, I resigned the church I pastored to help other churches and ministries invest their God-given talents. I have taught churches the concept of Small Groups and facilitated the implementation of those programs. At Bible Colleges, I have taught the concepts of leadership and the importance of knowing our calling, making our election sure. The drive behind much of my ministry stems from my knowledge of God's desire for His people to properly invest their talents in the kingdom, and for those talents to initiate growth. That is my passion.

It blesses me to see God's people invest His resources properly, and grieves me when they invest poorly. The burden and passion for this book comes from a deep concern that I have for God's wasted talents—talents of gifted people who never find their place of ministry. Talents of time and energy spent on projects that lose their glitter and fade after the excitement wears off. Talents of money poorly spent or squandered on projects that are soon forgotten…talents that God wants us to cultivate and grow, and not take lightly.

Yet, I've noticed a growing trend. Good churches with good people and pastors spend a lot of time, effort, and resources to start ministries in the church. But after limited—or even great success,—they drop the ministry to invest themselves elsewhere.

In the area of personal finance and investing, it is said that "dollar cost averaging" is the best way to invest. Namely, we should expect the greatest amount of growth to our investment if we stretch our deposits over a long period of time. That way, we take advantage of the market changes and protect ourselves from investing only when the market is at its highest.

The mistake most people make is that they allow their emotions to dictate, investing only when a fund or stock climbs. They buy the stock after it has already increased, rather than purchasing it before its assent. On the other hand, by dollar cost averaging over time—resisting emotional investing—a person buys the stock at its lowest point, and also as it climbs. In a bull market, stocks go up. By spacing your investments over time, as the market escalates, so will your stock's worth.

We all want our churches to grow; that is the fervent desire of every pastor or minister. We want it more than our next meal. Come on, we pray and fast for it to happen! We train and plan for it to happen. Everything within us yearns to see the kingdom of God advance within our given ministry.

But here is the mistake we make. Like an unwise investor, we get excited when we see other churches begin to grow. We watch them and try to imitate what they are doing to initiate that growth. We implement the same program or ministry. We do the same things they did. But when we experience little growth, we drop the whole plan to move on to the next "stock" that is climbing. This is replicated over a few weeks, months, and often years. In the process, we wasted time, people, energy, and the financial talents that were invested. Simply put, we buy as it's climbing and sell when it declines, but fail to realize the momentum building as it goes through its constant corrections toward a profit.

The kingdom of God is the best investment. I know it like I know my name. You do, too. Why else would you

Introduction

devote your life to it? Why else would you spend your time, energy, and life doing the work of God?

But we fail to understand momentum. We fail to realize the potential for growth when ministry or money is on the downslide. For instance, a stock's growth pattern has constant ups and downs. One minute the value of the stock soars; the next minute it plummets. In the same sense, programs, people, and ministries experience an up and down pattern toward growth.

Since the kingdom of God is the best investment, a penny dropped into an offering plate has unlimited potential and earnings power. In the same way, a minute working for God or a day invested in His kingdom will pay an eternal dividend. The growth pattern of God's kingdom is a bull pattern. It is increase. It is growth. It is profit.

I have seen, and so have you, churches experience growth through some of the craziest outreach programs. One church had tremendous numerical progress because they hand out turkeys in the park at Thanksgiving. Another church attributes the multiplied growth of their church to their cookie ministry. They simply distribute cookies to their neighbors. Other churches have bus ministries, small group ministries, and you-name-it ministries. The point is, God will use anything. Our position is to stay invested and not allow our emotions to decide when to start or release a ministry. Yes, there are times to buy and sell, but it is not when our emotions are at their highest. Emotions lie and are unreliable.

This book is dedicated to the burden and passion David Church and I have for the Body of Christ to understand momentum and its purpose in ministry. It is our prayer that you will understand ministry momentum as you never have before, and that you will discover how this law of God is present in all that we do for Him. Without it, chaos occurs. But with it, your ministry will experience the kind of growth and productivity that God requires of and desires for you, His investor.

One day we will hear, "Well done my good and faithful servant." Well done investor. Good job. You picked the right places and the right times to invest My talents and resources. Some of you may have a five-talent growth, and some will have a ten-talent growth. But there will be growth.

CHAPTER ONE

What is Momentum?

Momentum is a force more powerful than we realize and it greatly affects our lives. Yet it's not something that we consciously ponder or try to figure out. Scientists and physicists, however, study momentum all the time.

Momentum is defined as "mass in motion." All objects have mass; therefore, if an object of mass is moving then it has momentum. The amount of momentum an object has depends on two things:

1. The weight of the object that is moving.
2. The speed of the object that is moving.

In terms of an equation, the momentum of an object is equal to the mass of the object times the speed or velocity of the object. Momentum can also be measured by its direction. This is called linear momentum because now it has direction as well as magnitude.

Momentum occurs when a force that is greater than the resistance to the object is applied.

Momentum is a conserved quantity, meaning that the total momentum of any closed system (one not affected by outside forces) cannot change. Here on Earth, gravity is the outside force that comes to mind for most of us. Gravity is the force that gives weight to objects and mass on Earth. The Earth's mass creates a gravitational pull on all objects near its surface. Anything on or near the surface of the Earth such as planes, trains, and automobiles, <u>must use a force that is greater than gravity</u> for them to begin to move, and to keep moving. Once they are moving, they have created their own momentum. In order to sustain this momentum, <u>the forces that started that momentum must continue to operate, or momentum will decrease and eventually stop.</u>

> **As we address momentum in ministry, remember that it always takes an outside force for momentum to start, maintain, and to stop! In this book, we will address and discuss the outside forces that constantly threaten the continuance of momentum in the Church once momentum begins.**

Applications of Momentum

In sports, momentum is a term commonly used. We often hear things like, *"The Bears are gaining momentum,"* or *"The Blackhawks lost their momentum on the long road trip out west."* You may recall a situation like this: A team comes from behind and the coach calls a time out to give the team a pep talk. "Don't give up now," he urges. "You guys have the momentum, keep it up and you'll win this game!"

A team that has gained momentum is a team that is difficult to stop. Due to the power of momentum, teams with little talent sometimes defeat skilled and capable teams. Athletes with less ability usually have more heart and desire; therefore, experiencing a small taste of success is all they need to gain confidence. This confidence, combined with their passion to achieve, can build enough momentum in them and their game to defeat opponents who possess much more talent and skill.

Momentum also works in a reverse, negative manner. Just as small doses of success encourage a team, small amounts of failure discourages them. The most talented teams and athletes in the world fail due to a seed of doubt planted in their minds. When the negative momentum of failure is created, some force is needed to stop it; otherwise, a continuance of failure results.

(Dave's thoughts)

When I was growing up, grade-school math was a breeze for me. I loved it and made straight A pluses. In fact, I was selected as one of two students from sixth grade to represent our school at a special two-week program for gifted students. I couldn't figure out why some students could not understand the basics of math…it was so easy for me.

Then something happened in ninth grade. I had enrolled in the advanced mathematics class and my teacher, Mr. Elliot, was a brilliant mathematician. The problem was he overlooked some of the things going on in class. The class lacked discipline and soon a few students took advantage of it. We did whatever we wanted in class, and

Mr. Elliot just kept on teaching. Somehow, I got pulled into the class shenanigans and began to ignore the mathematician's instruction.

I learned Algebra the first semester and loved it. But I soon fell behind because I joined the class clowns. When the mid-semester exams came, I was nervous and rightly so. For the first time in my life I failed math. That shook my confidence but instead of trying to regroup and catch up, I thought I could turn it around on my own. In Algebra and almost all other areas of math, however, what you learn in one class is the foundation for the next.

I was too far behind to catch up and if it wasn't for my father meeting with my teacher that year, I would have failed ninth grade advanced mathematics. As it was, I barely squeaked by with a D minus.

From that year forward, I never again enrolled in an advanced math class. I excelled in the regular class, but I have always wondered what could have been if I had kept the momentum going. Eight years of positive momentum in math was ruined in a half semester because I got sidetracked and lost my confidence and momentum.

The Force of Momentum

Momentum is a powerful force. Just as momentum works in the natural world, momentum in ministry works in our ministries and spiritual lives. Yet, it is rarely talked about. Recognizing and understanding momentum will help us to advance the kingdom of God.

(Jim's thoughts)

I've been involved in ministry for over 25 years. During those years, I've participated in and been engaged in every area of church ministry including the pastorate. However, in the last six years my ministry has turned toward helping pastors in the area of church growth, and mentoring and developing their leadership teams.

When I began working with pastors and their leadership I was enthused. It amazes me what is possible in the church when people realize their true calling and begin to work together under their pastor's vision and directive.

This was exactly what I felt the Lord had been calling me to do for many years. Yet, after working closely with some of these churches, I became discouraged—not because of what I was doing because I loved the idea of bringing leadership teams closer to their pastors' visions as well as seeing individuals reach their full potentials. What discouraged me was the loss of momentum I observed some time after I left those churches.

Typically, when the pastor and I felt that the church and/or leadership were in the right position, I moved on to the next church. In the months following my departure, however, a loss of momentum invariably occurred. Once my individual passion and energy was removed, the ministry began to decline.

What I had failed to realize when I worked with those local assemblies was that I was the motivating force. My calling, my energy, my vision were all working behind the scenes to cause momentum in a particular area of ministry in those churches.

I had spent nearly six years in this type of ministry, only to see much of those efforts fall to the wayside once I left. That disappointment was one of the primary elements that ignited my passion for this book.

Over and over again, the loss of momentum takes place in churches daily all around the world. This loss causes untold disappointment and frustration. A minister with great passion and vision will experience only so many disappointments and frustrations before they succumb to discouragement, even doubting themselves and their calling.

Whether it is a job or a ministry, we must realize that it takes effort or force to create that job or ministry. Someone has to think it through. Somebody has to organize and put all the pieces together. Somebody has to create a system of action that will propel the ministry forward. Then someone must assume the position to maintain that ministry. Without that person, momentum will decline.

Momentum: Maintenance and Resistance

New ideas excite us. Most ministers are enthusiastic about new ministries. We love to hear success stories because they encourage us to try the same things in our own churches. We go to conferences and hear another pastor talk about the great success or growth within his/her church. Excitedly, we listen as the minister explains how and why that growth occurred. Eager about the possibilities for our own ministries, we return home and tell our leaders and congregations what we learned.

But here's the problem: If someone—lacking the vision and burden to create the momentum—tries to *duplicate* someone else's success it often fails. Why? Because that person may lack the energy and passion it takes to *create and maintain* the kind of momentum the first person had. As a result, they soon become discouraged in their efforts and in the new area of ministry. This causes a loss of interest and soon the momentum that was initially created is lost along with the investment of time and energy.

Those of you who have been in the ministry for any length of time realize how hard it is to gain the support of your congregation for a single thought or new idea. You know that people seldom get on board with a new vision immediately. It takes months, and sometimes even years, for an entire congregation to get behind its pastor or leadership team's vision for a church. Experts claim that it takes almost six years for an individual to feel as if the pastor is *their* pastor. Given that statistic, how much longer does it take for the whole congregation to get behind that pastor's passion and vision for the church?

Yes, good oratory moves people. During the sermon, folks get excited. As the pastor explains the new vision or area of ministry he would like to implement in the church, congregants will clap their hands and say "Yes!" and "Amen!" to everything. Yet in the months following, a pastor realizes that his or her congregation wasn't as supportive as he/she originally thought.

People are emotional; however, work (the force) is seldom accomplished through emotions. Work is accomplished when people make a conscious decision to help implement change in their churches or communities. Only when a person makes a conscious decision to support the leadership, will they do whatever it takes to maintain the momentum in that particular ministry. They will give financially. They will give of their time. They will give of their talent and they will continue to give until they are either told to stop, or until something happens that causes resistance to the momentum.

With that in mind, let's examine a few of the causes that create resistance to momentum:

- **A new pastor.** Reports claim that the average tenure of a pastor is only a few years. How sad when you consider that it takes years to rally the congregation to move in the direction of obtaining momentum. Often, a new pastor brings his own passion and vision; he must take the church in the direction he feels God is leading. In the process, the already existing ministries that are currently experiencing positive momentum, are soon overlooked and neglected.

- **A leader in a ministry position moves away.** Whenever someone involved in a ministry moves away, a replacement has to be trained. If the new person is trained improperly or lacks passion, their involvement will decline and so will that ministry. As a result, a struggle occurs for the ministry to continue as we apply pressure to train, mentor, and encourage that individual.

- **New people move into the church.** As new people come into the church, it is important they find a place of ministry quickly. Every person needs to feel they are a vital part of their church's vision for growth. Given that, we are constantly trying to find places of ministry in which people can serve. Sometimes we place new people in a ministry that someone else has labored in for years. Often, we place them as an assistant or as a substitute in the person's absence. Depending on the individuals' personalities, this can either be a good or bad situation. If petty jealousies start, then the disagreements and lack of cooperation often derail that ministry.

<u>Every ministry must have a force greater than the resistance behind it.</u> That includes regular and consistent meetings between the pastor and heads of ministry. Those meetings should include regular times of training, teaching and prayer. Some type of mentoring program should also be in place. Without this constant force, momentum will soon be lost.

Establish Consistency and a System

(Jim's thoughts)

I don't do well managing something if I have to repeat the same things each day. I like change. I like new challenges. I like finding problems and solving them. Yet I appreciate people who are capable of doing the same thing over and over every day. Once a system is created they are quite capable of maintaining that system for months or even years. Some men spend their entire careers pulling the same lever over and over again. I can appreciate that, but I'm not like that.

Most of us love to start projects, yet many of us dislike finishing them. Are you one of those? *You know who you are!* The pitfall of people like this is that momentum in ministry is never realized or maintained. People who start things and don't finish them are often good at rallying others. They stand on their soapbox and get everybody shouting for change. They even have some idea of what the change should be, but when they realize the need for constant force they soon move on to the next soapbox idea.

If you are in ministry you are probably moved by and sensitive to the leading of the Holy Spirit. You are also a person who is capable of birthing a vision. For these two reasons, it is very easy for you to hear from God and get motivated about what God wants to accomplish. Yet, it is important to realize that God seldom, if ever, works on our timetable.

(Jim's thoughts)

In my years of ministry I have learned that when God gives me a vision it is not for the immediate but rather for years down the road. What's more, God often speaks to me about something that He doesn't even want me to do. Just as we'll share a secret with a close friend, God often shares His plan with someone for no other reason than to show them what He desires to accomplish. Just because God shares His plan, doesn't mean that He necessarily wants you to implement it. God may want to use someone near to you to accomplish what He has revealed. Perhaps your role is to encourage or mentor that person to equip him/her for the task.

I realize that although the vision is clear and needful, it is not always for me to do. For that reason, it is vitally important that we—as God's ministers—learn to temper ourselves in the areas of casting vision. <u>*Remember, the Spirit is always subject to the prophet.*</u>

I, like you, have seen too many visions cast only to fall away. Wouldn't you rather see half as many visions cast in order to see a greater percentage of them realized?

It is time that we stop talking about doing things and actually do them. We preachers are too good at motivating people about a vision. Ashamedly, I admit that at times I have stood behind a pulpit and cast a vision to the congregation. Months or weeks later, after realizing how difficult the vision was to maintain, I cast a new vision and moved on to something else. When we do this, we waste the energies and the efforts that were used to create the first momentum. In essence, we wasted God's resources.

People are not as expendable as we think. A lack of results wearies them especially after they invest their time, energy and money to support their pastor's and leadership team's vision.

We rarely hear their discouragement. They seldom stand up and tell you they are unhappy with your decision to abandon a ministry in which they invested themselves. However, the next time you cast a vision, those people will be reluctant to come on board. It's not easy to move people. It's even harder to move them a second time. It is almost impossible to move them if they feel you are wasting their time, energy or money.

(Jim's thoughts)

When I graduated from high school in the early '80's, the country was in a bad recession. The recession was especially felt in the steel mills of northwest Indiana, where I grew up. The only job I could find was at McDonald's. I can't tell you how silly I felt wearing that fast-food-chain's uniform. But I'm so glad I did. Yes, McDonald's taught me how to cook hamburgers and quarter pounders and fish fillets, but it also taught me the essentials about systems.

Have you ever noticed that teenagers pretty much run McDonald's restaurants? Did you also notice that the hamburgers from all locations taste pretty much the same? And teenagers made them!

Let's face it, parents can't get their teens to take out the garbage much of the time, let alone maintaining the kind of systems consistency that a large world-wide corporation like McDonald's would require. McDonald's Corporation has perfected the art of creating systems and implementing them.

When I worked at McDonald's, they escorted me to the fryer that made the chicken sandwiches and step-by-step they explained how a chicken sandwich should be made. Timers went off when the buns were toasted and devices dispensed an exact amount of sauce on each sandwich. Any teenager could make that sandwich because it was made the same way in every McDonald's restaurant around the world.

McDonald's created a system and then employed people to continue and repeat that system whether they cook hamburgers or fries, or clean the parking lot. It's all about consistency, implementing the job you were trained to do.

In the church, we have ministries, not jobs. Nevertheless, there are certain things we must do to ensure that the ministry continues and maintains momentum.

In the church, we often lack systems. We allow people to do whatever they want because we lack the training or understanding to make that ministry move forward. This is a prescription for chaos and it creates a dysfunctional church.

Church leaders must learn what it takes for a ministry to maintain and increase momentum. If the pastor is inexperienced in a given ministry, he should find an experienced person to create a system within the church and then train, teach, and mentor those involved in that ministry.

Just because the pastor knows nothing about music, does not mean that the church can't have an awesome music ministry. Just because the pastor has no connection with youth, does not mean that the church must forego an incredible youth ministry.

Although the pastor may lack the ability to put that music department together or cause the youth ministry to grow, it is within his ability to find someone who has the expertise and abilities to create and maintain those types of ministries.

In Conclusion

Remember—Momentum occurs when a force that is greater than the resistance to the object is applied.

The value of applying force to an object to create momentum is not so much the force itself; rather, it is when, how, and where to apply that force. Don't feel inadequate if you're not the direct force behind a ministry. Directing the force behind a ministry creates an even greater influence when it is applied correctly. A force alone can cause something to go in a wrong or dangerous direction. However, if you have the ability to direct and encourage that force behind the object, you have something of genuine purpose and you *will* create momentum.

CHAPTER TWO

God's Nature

Genesis 1:1-2

> 1 In the beginning God created the Heaven and the earth.
>
> 2 And the earth was without form, and void; and darkness was upon the face of the deep. **And the Spirit of God moved upon the face of the waters.**

The Bible describes the Earth as a mass of emptiness in the beginning. No form. No light. No movement. The Message Bible calls it a "soup of nothingness." But when God moved, everything changed. Most of us know the story of creation, but few of us consider the momentum that God created in that first six-day period.

When God moves, the movement remains. The Bible says that God's Word is forever settled. When He speaks something into existence, it will always exist unless He ordains otherwise. His Word is constant, unchanging and eternal. That is the essence of momentum; namely, God's very nature and everything He does, creates and moves with momentum.

When God formed man from the dust of the earth, He breathed into his nostrils the breath of life and man became a living soul. But why do we keep breathing? What causes that?

We breathe today not because of some Big Bang theory, but because God breathed into us the breath of life and has ordained life to continue and flourish on this Earth. From one man and one woman to 7 billion people in the space of 6,000 years...that is God-created momentum!

God spoke into existence every kind of tree, grass, plant, fruit and vegetable, and He placed its own seed within itself. The Scripture reads...

Genesis 1:11-12

> 11 And God said, Let the earth bring forth grass, the herb yielding seed, and the fruit tree yielding fruit after his kind, whose seed is in itself, upon the earth: and it was so.
>
> 12 And the earth brought forth grass, and herb yielding seed after his kind, and the tree yielding fruit, **whose seed was in itself,** after his kind: and God saw that it was good.

God saw that it was good, and all of the plant life that was in the Earth began to grow.

Genesis 2:5

> 5 And every plant of the field before it was in the earth, and every herb of the field before it **grew:**

Every living thing still grows to this day because God ordained it. The seed keeps reproducing after its kind year after year, season after season. God is a God of momentum; everything He touches in creation keeps moving and growing and is still bringing new life. The fish of the sea, the fowls of the air, the cattle, the beast of the Earth, and every creeping thing on the

Earth are still alive and multiplying today because God commanded them to "be fruitful and multiply."

Consider how God created the Sun and Moon; one rules by day, the other rules by night. When He did this, He set the Earth in orbital motion around the Sun and the Moon in orbit around the Earth.

Genesis 1:14-16

> 14 And God said, Let there be lights in the firmament of the heaven to divide the day from the night; **and let them be for signs, and for seasons, and for days, and years:**
>
> 15 And let them be for lights in the firmament of the heaven to give light upon the earth: and it was so.
>
> 16 And **God made two great lights; the greater light to rule the day, and the lesser light to rule the night:** he made the stars also.

Days, nights, months, years, seasons of cold and warmth and wet and dry exist today because God set the Earth in perpetual motion 6,000 years ago. The rivers, the wind and the natural resources that God spoke into existence at creation, are creating momentum for mankind today through gas, oil, and electricity for our everyday needs.

THE FORCE OF GOD'S NATURE IN GRAVITY

When we think of gravity, momentum comes to mind. The Sun's gravity keeps the Earth in orbit around the Sun, and the Earth's gravity keeps the Moon in orbit around the Earth. One could argue that it is gravity itself that keeps the Earth moving around the Sun and that's true; however, God's momentum enables everything to move in order for gravity to exist.

For many years, NASA and others have used gravity to assist the flight of their spacecrafts in outer space. The gravity of the Earth, Moon, or any other celestial body can be utilized to alter the path and the speed of a spacecraft. This is known as the gravitational slingshot, or a gravity assist. The assist is provided by the angular momentum of the planet as it pulls the spacecraft. During a space flight, gravity actually can be used to accelerate or decelerate a spacecraft.

During one of NASA's early flights to the Moon in 1970, the Apollo 13 used a gravity assist from the Moon to transport it back to Earth before they ran out of oxygen. Many gravity assists have been used since that time to send spacecraft beyond the Moon even as far as Saturn.

Gravity also affects the rivers, lakes, and oceans causing them to flow and drain in certain directions. Oceans have currents that are generated by the Earth's rotation, the wind, and the gravitational pull of the Sun and Moon. The oceanic currents travel around the entire planet and have done so since the beginning of time and still continue today.

The Conservation of Linear Momentum in Ministry

For a moment, let's explore man's scientific law of momentum. This law is called the Conservation of Linear Momentum. This fundamental law of nature states that the total momentum

God's Nature

of a closed system of objects (which has no interactions with external agents) is constant. One of the consequences of this is that the center of mass of any system of objects will always continue with the same velocity unless acted on by a force from outside the system.

Using that information, consider the spiritual aspects of this law in regard to ministry momentum. If ministry takes the place of one of the objects mentioned above, God has set ministry in this world. He intends for it to continue and to prosper in every church, city, village or hamlet and no force should come against it to lose its velocity. That is what He has ordained.

Matthew 16:18
> And I say also unto thee, That thou art Peter, and upon this rock I will build my church; and the gates of hell shall not prevail against it.

God has empowered each church to go forward and continue regardless of outside influences or forces that would try to stop it. Its velocity has been established.

God will have a Church without spot or wrinkle. He will have a Bride. Regardless of what the world does or says, nothing can stop His church. You and I can work to see it happen or we can work against it. In either case, the end result will be the same. The church will continue with or without us, with our help or without it, because of us or despite us. Why? Because God has already set it in motion and directed its constant momentum since His Spirit first moved upon the face of the deep.

God is a God of momentum. The first mention of Him in the Bible describes Him creating, moving and speaking life into existence. He moved upon the face of the deep and caused oceanic currents to begin and continue to this day. He breathed the breath of life into the nostrils of mankind and caused them to become a living, eternal soul.

Just as the entire universe moves and breathes based on the momentum God established in the beginning, so does the church. It is His nature to start something and allow it to continue for as long as He wills.

God is the same, yesterday, today and forever. You are part of His family, and you can experience momentum in your ministry because God desires it to be so. He spoke it and it is established. Receive that promise today!

CHAPTER THREE

God Will Have a People

When God decides to do something, nothing can stop Him. In creation, God moved on the face of the waters and nothing could stop that movement. With His spoken Word, the Lord started a spiritual momentum that created light, the heavens and the Earth, and all living things including man. As we have discussed in the previous chapter, when God speaks something into existence, it happens!

Among all the things that God created, He created man in His own image. He did so to have a relationship with us. That was His utmost desire at creation—to fellowship with man.

Revelation 4:11
> 11 Thou art worthy, O Lord, to receive glory and honour and power: **for thou hast created all things, and for thy pleasure they are and were created.**

Although we were created for the express purpose of fellowshipping with our Creator, God also made us free agents with the freedom and ability to choose right or wrong. Every relationship takes two people to participate and it is no different in our relationship with God. He gives us the choice to interact with Him or not.

Adam chose to eat from the forbidden tree and reaped the consequences of disobedience. As a result, sin entered into the world and corrupted mankind. Yet even though Adam failed, God still desired to cultivate a relationship with man, yearning for a people who would worship and obey Him.

In his generation, Noah was a perfect man. He found grace in the sight of God and through this one man and his family, the Lord would choose His people and continue His work. In a sense, Noah became a prototype of the second Adam. Mankind failed the first time because of bad choices, so God continued His momentum through another man, Noah. God always has a people.

God's relationship with man was a safety net our Creator instituted to guarantee that His plan would advance. Even His anger and wrath could not stop the momentum that He had established. Just as gravity holds the Earth in place, God's relationship with mankind secures the momentum of His divine will for His people.

Through Noah's descendants came Abram, a man of faith who desired a relationship with God. When the Lord saw that Abram's heart was upright and open to Him God said: "This is the man through whom I will continue to work. This is the family that I will bless. From this family will come My people."

God's Covenant with Abraham

God made a covenant with Abraham saying,

Genesis 13:16
> 16 And I will make thy seed as the dust of the earth: so that if a man can number the dust of the earth, then shall thy seed also be numbered.

No one can number the dust of the Earth; hence the seed of Abraham, father of the nation of Israel, flourishes today because of God's spoken Word! For thousands of years, nations have tried to destroy Israel but failed because God declared that His chosen nation will number as the dust of the Earth.

Amazingly, much of Israel's growth occurred after Jacob and his family moved to Egypt to escape the famine. It was then that God reaffirmed His covenant with him...

Genesis 46:3
> 3 And he said, I am God, the God of thy father: fear not to go down into Egypt; **for I will there make of thee a great nation:**

All was well with Jacob when he moved his entire family of seventy to Egypt. The Pharaoh allowed them to live in the land of Goshen—the best property in Egypt— and the family "grew exceedingly" in that land.

Time passed and Jacob, Joseph, and that entire generation died. Still, the Israelites "waxed exceedingly mighty" in the land of Egypt. Meanwhile, a new Pharaoh assumed power. The new leader worried that Israel would exceed Egypt in greatness and eventually would fight against them. So he enslaved God's people and set taskmasters over them to build bricks that were used to construct massive cities for Pharaoh. Even then, God's people kept growing.

Exodus 1:12

> 12 But the more they afflicted them, the more they multiplied and grew. And they were grieved because of the children of Israel.

Desperate and afraid, Pharaoh decreed that every newborn son must die and only the daughters would live. In doing so, Pharaoh tried to control the population; but his plan failed. God had promised that Israel would number as the sand of the sea and she would thrive in Egypt.

For a period of 400 years, God's people were enslaved and labored in Egypt, yet they still grew exponentially. During the Exodus from Egypt they numbered some 2.5 million people, almost as many as the entire Egyptian population of that day! When God chooses to set something in motion it will happen... Momentum at its best!

The Numbering of Israel

The Bible records the exact number of men in Israel who were able to fight at the time of the Exodus.

Numbers 1:44-47

> 44 These are those that were numbered, which Moses and Aaron numbered, and the princes of Israel, being twelve men: each one was for the house of his fathers.
>
> 45 So were all those that were numbered of the children of Israel, by the house of their fathers, **from twenty years old and upward, all that were able to go forth to war in Israel;**
>
> 46 Even all they that were numbered were **six hundred thousand and three thousand and five hundred and fifty.**
>
> 47 But the Levites after the tribe of their fathers were not numbered among them.

At first count, the twelve tribes of Israel numbered 603, 550 men of fighting age. This did not include males under 20-years-old or any from the tribe of Levi. That's a huge army of men considering the time and the size of the Jewish people. In comparison, America only has about twice that number in her armed forces today.

Larry Booker, author of *"What a Difference a Line Can Make,"* gives an interesting and thoughtful study of the Book of Numbers. He shares some of Israel's population numbers, relating stories behind those figures.

In his book, Larry noted that none of these men or their families entered the Promised Land except for Joshua and Caleb. For 40 years, these fighting men and their families lived, gave birth, and died in the desert. However, one would expect that their growth rate would continue. After all, they flourished for 400 years enslaved in Egypt. Instead, this generation was cursed with plague after plague and setback after setback:

- In Chapter 11, a plague struck Israel for lusting after quail.
- In Chapter 16, the sons of Levi rose up against Moses and Aaron only for the earth to swallow them alive.
- When the congregation blamed Moses for their deaths, God cursed them with a plague.
- In Chapter 21, God sent a plague of fiery serpents because the people were speaking against Moses and Aaron.
- In Chapter 25, the people suffered another plague because they ate meat sacrificed to the Moabite gods.

Finally, when the last one died God commanded the people to number the tribes one more time before they enter the Promised Land.

What can we learn from this?

The twelve tribes of Israel now numbered 601,730 men of fighting age.

They lost 1,820 men over the 40 years since the last numbering. That may not seem like much, but if 70 people grew to 3 million in 400 years, God's people should have grown at least 10 percent in those 40 years—that would equal 300,000 more people!. After all, they had more advantages in the wilderness than they had in Egypt.

- They were no longer slaves.
- They no longer toiled every day to build huge buildings.
- Their clothes did not wear out.
- They had all the food and water they needed.

But instead of increasing, they decreased in number by 1,820 fighting men. It looked like God's covenant with Abraham was no longer in effect. Growth stopped and they actually began to decrease. It appeared as if the momentum of God's spoken Word was gone. So what happened?

Remember Israel was divided into twelve tribes.

Some tribes grew in number while others decreased; some grew rapidly, while others incurred great losses.

For instance:
- Manasseh increased 20,500.
- Ephraim lost 8,000.
- Benjamin gained 10,200.
- Reuben lost 2,770.
- Asher grew by 11,900 men.

The most shocking statistic of all is the tribe of Simeon, who lost 37,100 fighting men. It was as if God rolled up His sleeve, drew back his fist, and slew them! Simeon started out as one of the largest tribes, but was now by far the smallest. Although all twelve tribes were Israelites, each tribe had its own characteristics, differences, and prophecies concerning their futures.

Larry Booker's book focused on the tribes who had *lost* the most men, but let's focus on a few tribes who *gained* the most; namely, Manasseh and Asher.

God promised that He would still have a people, **but it would be a people who obeyed Him.** The Lord cannot bless disobedience so He transferred his promise from Simeon and

Ephraim, to Manasseh, Benjamin, and Asher. The promise would come through them.

1 Corinthians 10:5

> **5 But with many of them God was not well pleased:** for they were overthrown in the wilderness.

What did Manasseh do that was right? And what caused Asher to grow so much during this time? Manasseh and Ephraim were not sons of Jacob as the other ten tribes were; rather, they were Joseph's sons, the grandsons of Jacob. But Jacob blessed them as he had his other sons so the covenant of promise also applied to them.

Genesis 48:20

> 20 And he blessed them that day, saying, In thee shall Israel bless, saying, God make thee as Ephraim and as Manasseh: and he set Ephraim before Manasseh.

THE TRIBE OF MANASSEH

The tribe of Manasseh had no part in the rebellion against Moses and Aaron at the tabernacle. In fact, the daughters of Manasseh stood up for the rights of families that had no sons to inherit the possessions of their father.

Manasseh was the only tribe to settle on both sides of the Jordan. As a result, this tribe played a prominent part in the defeat of the natives on both sides of the river. Two of the greatest battles that Israel ever won were won by mighty men from the tribe of Manasseh. Both Gideon, who defeated the Midianites with a small army, and Jepthah, who defeated the Ammonites in a miraculous and victorious battle, belonged to the tribe of Manasseh.

Manasseh obeyed God and drove out the enemies whenever they were called to do so, while some of the others chose not to fight. God saw something in Manasseh that the other tribes lacked; namely, a willingness to stand up and fight for what God had promised them. As a result, God was well pleased with their faith in His promises.

The Tribe of Asher

The tribe of Asher was also blessed with great growth. Moses prophesied that Asher would be blessed with children, and Jacob prophesied that Asher would become famous for rich foods and sweets fit for a king. History reveals that the lands of Asher were so fertile that crops grew more abundantly there than in any other place. What's more, their fields provided all of Israel with olive oil.

Why was Asher so blessed in population and prosperity? Rabbinical literature explains that, for a time, Asher was on bad terms with his brothers. Asher informed his brothers of Reuben's sin against his stepmother, Bilhah, but they disbelieved him and held him in reproach. Regardless of the pressure from his brothers, Asher stood firm and eventually Rueben confessed and repented of his sin. But from the onset, Asher held no evil intent against his brothers. Instead, he desired to reconcile them as one family. The Scriptures regard Asher as a virtuous man who only strived for good; consequently, his descendants were blessed because of him.

These examples reveal how God kept His promises alive and moving forward through those who were obedient to Him. When God sets His plan in motion, it comes to fruition because His Word is "forever settled in heaven."

The Lord will actually pick and choose specific tribes or people who are obedient to Him to fulfill His divine plan. Obedience is fundamental and a precursor to receiving God's blessings because "obedience is better than sacrifice." And God's momentum is sustained through obedience to His Holy Word!

Consider Israel's more recent population growth...

For a period of approximately 3,300 years, from the Exodus until 1850 AD, Israel's population remained nearly unchanged. Different history books vary on these numbers, but the nation fluctuated between 2 to 4 million people. Israel's momentum of growth ceased and her people were eventually exiled from their homeland. For the most part, the people disobeyed God's Word and refused to accept Jesus as the Messiah. For 2,000 years they wandered and settled in places that were not their own. Eventually, their population scattered over the entire world.

Then toward the middle of the nineteenth century, Israel began to increase. From that time until they became a nation in 1948, their population grew from about 3 million to approximately 16 million people. This growth occurred despite the murder of 5 million Jews by Stalin and 6 million killed by Hitler. Had this not occurred, 30 million Jewish people would populate the Earth.

Clearly, God blessed His people despite severe persecution. The crimes of humanity against God's people so grieved Him that perhaps He wanted to let the world know that He will always have a people—Israel.

There are literally hundreds of books that document the stories of nations that have come against Israel. Nations have attacked her since the ancient days of Egypt in an attempt to banish Israel from the face of the Earth. But God will never allow His people to be destroyed! Why? Because God's Word is forever settled and He is a God of momentum.

God's Church

God will always have a people and God will always have a church.

Matthew 16:18
> 18 And I say also unto thee, That thou art Peter, **and upon this rock I will build my church; and the gates of hell shall not prevail against it.**

Despite devils, demons, sickness and disease, God will have His people, His Church. War cannot stop it. Hell cannot stop it. Even God's own anger could not stop it because His relationship with man establishes a momentum that is unstoppable.

Acts 5:39
> 39 **But if it be of God, ye cannot overthrow it;** lest haply ye be found even to fight against God.

God set His Church in motion at Pentecost 2,000 years ago, and it has moved forward ever since.

Israel's history foreshadowed events that the New Testament church would face. The Church would suffer persecution, just as

Israel did, yet she would persevere and endure to the end. At times it looked as if Satan would gain the upper hand, but he failed because God and His Church are more than conquerors.

The gates of Hell cannot prevail against the Church because the force behind it is stronger than the force that is against it. The gravitational pull of sin has no hold on her. The "weight of sin that doth so easily beset us" no longer pertains if we live according to God's Word.

There is no question, God will have a church. The only question is who is the Church? "Whosoever will, let him come..." Those who are obedient to His Word will be a part of this unstoppable momentum. Those who do not, will fall prey to the enemy and the weight of sin. It is a personal decision we must all make.

Will You Be The Church?

Isn't it amazing how swiftly the Israelites forgot the powerful miracles God performed on their behalf? They murmured and complained that they were better off in Egypt, where they backslid and worshipped idols. The Bible records instances when God, intolerant of and angered with His people, sent plagues upon them. Shortly after, they would repent and Moses would plead their cause. Then God in His mercy and love would withhold His judgment.

Had Israel chosen to believe in God's promises, she could have avoided multiple sufferings and needless wandering in the wilderness for 40 years. But Israel's discontentment fueled her unbelief. The people wanted to establish roots and enjoy life instead of traveling through the desert.

In the same manner, life gets the better of us sometimes. We get busy and the cares of this world distract us. We become immersed in the world and in the process, we forget our purpose, our calling. We lose sight of how far God has brought us. Discontented, we focus on our problems instead of God's promises and without realizing it, we begin to serve the gods of this world and fall away from God. We don't plan to backslide, it just happens.

That is why it is important to make conscious choices every day. We must think about Whom we serve and what we believe. Then we must act on those beliefs.

After Joshua led Israel into the Promised Land and conquered Jericho and the Kings of Canaan, he gathered the tribes of Israel together. He called all of the elders of Israel and the judges with their officers to Shechem for a final word before he died.

Joshua reminded them that they possessed their Promised Land. Every tribe had a territory and had received an inheritance. Every tribe had fields, houses, and land. He reminded them that God had kept His promise to Abraham, Isaac and Jacob. He reminded them that they were part of this promise, and now they were finally home.

Joshua said, "Take a look around. You are living in a land you did not labor for. You're living in cities that you did not build and you are eating from vineyards that you did not plant." Joshua reminded them and wanted them to be cognizant that God came through for them and their fathers.

This was the younger generation of Israel and Joshua was very old. In fact, he was the only one remaining from the days in Egypt. All the others had died never receiving the promise. So Joshua recounted their history to the younger generation, reminding them how their fathers had fallen away from God and served idols. At the same time, he admonished them to serve the Lord with all their hearts. He said...

Joshua 24:14-15

> 14 Now therefore fear the Lord, and serve him in sincerity and in truth: and put away the gods which your fathers served on the other side of the flood, and in Egypt; and serve ye the Lord.
>
> 15 And if it seem evil unto you to serve the Lord, **choose you this day whom ye will serve**; whether the gods which your fathers served that were on the other side of the flood, or the gods of the Amorites, in whose land ye dwell: **but as for me and my house, we will serve the Lord.**

Joshua insisted that the Israelites choose either the one true God, or false gods. No more messing around. It must have been a sobering moment, yet the question demanded an answer. It required a response and this is what they said:

Joshua 24:16-21

> 16 And the people answered and said, God forbid that we should forsake the Lord, to serve other gods;
>
> 17 For the Lord our God, he it is that brought us up and our fathers out of the land of Egypt, from the house of bondage, and which did those great signs in our sight, and preserved us in all the way wherein we went, and among all the people through whom we passed:
>
> 18 And the Lord drove out from before us all the people, even the Amorites which dwelt in the land: **therefore will we also serve the Lord; for he is our God.**

Notice how they put it, "We will also serve the Lord." It was as if they were saying, "We will serve our father's gods and we will also serve the Lord." That ticked off Joshua.

> 19 And Joshua said unto the people, Ye cannot serve the Lord: for he is a holy God; he is a jealous God; he will not forgive your transgressions nor your sins.
> 20 If ye forsake the Lord, and serve strange gods, then he will turn and do you hurt, and consume you, after that he hath done you good.
> 21 And the people said unto Joshua, **Nay; but we will serve the Lord.**

When the people finally chose to serve the Lord, Joshua declared them as witnesses against themselves, and they agreed. So under the giant oak tree in Shechem, Joshua made a covenant with the people that day. He set a great stone near God's sanctuary as a witness to the people, indicating that the stone heard every word spoken. This witness was for their generation and all future generations as a reminder to never deny God.

Joshua died soon after that, yet the promise continued because a generation of people understood the importance of choice.

Joshua 24:31

> 31 And Israel served the Lord all the days of Joshua, **and all the days of the elders that overlived Joshua,** and which had known all the works of the Lord, that he had done for Israel.

In Conclusion

Who do you choose to serve today? Are you God's own…are you His Church? Will you choose to stay in His will? When you choose the Living God you choose life. God's promises will manifest in your life, extending into your children's lives for generations to come.

It is forever settled that God will have a people, a church, to bring glory to His Name. When God starts a work, He completes it because the force behind the work is stronger than the resistance against it. That is God's very nature! God is a God of momentum! But if we depart from God's plan for our lives, our own sin and self-centeredness barricades the flow of momentum.

Stay in God's will. Commit yourself to pray and fast and God will strengthen and equip you to stand against the resisting forces that would destroy the momentum in your ministry and life.

> *Remember, God wants you to succeed as part of His Church. He has set the Church in motion, and it cannot be stopped. People will come against you, Satan will try and have his way, but if you stay in God's Church you and your ministry will prevail!*

CHAPTER FOUR

Creating Momentum: A New Thing

The easiest and most obvious way to create momentum is to start something new. Everyone loves "new and improved." Although there are various facets of introducing something new, when we think of new in the ministry the first thing that comes to mind is new music or a new song.

The Psalmist David said:

Psalm 33:3-4

> 3 **Sing unto him a new song;** play skilfully with a loud noise.
> 4 For the word of the Lord is right; and all his works are done in truth.

Psalm 98:1

> 98 **O sing unto the Lord a new song;** for he hath done marvellous things: his right hand, and his holy arm, hath gotten him the victory.

Throughout his life, David did his best to compose a new song in praise to the Lord. The Book of Psalms is filled with these music accolades to God. Many considered this a sign of David's deep love for God and His wonderful works. True enough, yet David had other reasons for His musical expressions of praise.

1 Samuel 16:23

> 23 And it came to pass, when the evil spirit from God was upon Saul, that **David took an harp, and played with his hand:** so Saul was refreshed, and was well, and the evil spirit departed from him.

After God rejected King Saul for repeated rebellion, He troubled him with an evil spirit. As a means of comfort and assistance, King Saul called on David to play the harp for him. When Saul heard the soothing sounds of the harp, the Bible records that the evil spirit departed and Saul was refreshed and well.

The Bible doesn't disclose if David's songs were new, but in all probability they were new to King Saul. David understood that music was one of the most powerful forces on the face of the Earth. It has the power to liberate people from the bondages they face in life.

Psalm 40:3

> 3 And he hath **put a new song in my mouth**, even praise unto our God: **many shall see it, and fear, and shall trust in the Lord.**

David noted from experience that new songs and music would cause many to turn toward God. Consider the occasions when guests in your church turned to God during the worship service before the preaching ever started. The first time someone hears Pentecostal music, it literally breaks down walls of fear and doubt and ushers them into the presence of Almighty God.

God uses music to draw sinners to Himself. Yet sadly, regular church-goers, who are familiar with the songs and manner of worship, often become too acclimated. For them, the music turns mundane. Yet, a new song of praise will do the same for them as it did for that person who visited church for the very first time.

(Dave's Comments)

My wife is our music leader and she always searches for the next new song. She travels to music conferences, scours music stores, and listens to music on the Internet all because she wants to please the Lord with a new song.

Nothing gets a Pentecostal church service moving like a new song! Every week or two she introduces something fresh, and the church catches on fire. Often the move of God is so strong that people are filled with the Holy Ghost and lives are changed before the preacher ever preaches.

The Psalmist states that new music restores the fear of the Lord and causes many to trust in God. That is momentum. God is pleased with music that gives glory to Him; it creates momentum in the service that draws people into worship. There is something about a new song of praise that creates excitement and momentum in a church—and in the hearts of people—like nothing else does.

Of course, new doesn't necessarily guarantee momentum. A new idea must be a noticeable improvement over the old idea.

People have to be able to see the difference for themselves. If they can't see it, feel it, touch or taste it then it's not an improvement at all.

The corporate world has been using the "new and improved" method of marketing for many years now, and it still works well today.

New Coca-Cola: New and Improved?

A great example of this is the story of the popular soft drink company, Coca-Cola. Perhaps you remember when Coca-Cola decided to bring out their "New Coke" in the late eighties. The story goes something like this...

> Just after World War II, the market share for the Coca-Cola Company's flagship beverage was 52 percent, and in 1983 it had shrunk to under 24 percent in the face of competition from Pepsi-Cola. Pepsi had begun to outsell Coke in supermarkets and Coke maintained its edge only through fountain sales.
>
> Market analysts believed baby boomers were likely to purchase more diet drinks as they aged and remained health and weight conscious. Therefore, any future growth in the full-calorie segment had to come from younger drinkers who, at that time, favored Pepsi and its sweetness by even more overwhelming margins than the market as a whole.
>
> When Roberto Goizueta took over as CEO in 1980, he pointedly told employees there would be no sacred cows in how the company did its business, including how it formulated its drinks.

Creating Momentum: A New Thing

So they began testing new formulas on focus groups in taste tests around the country. Many of these surveys showed that people would indeed buy this "New Coke." On April 23, 1985, Coca-Cola stopped production of their original drink and released the new version.

Protestors started to complain and threatened to not drink Coke again because it wasn't the same and it wasn't better. They wanted their old drink back. Though a few loved the new version, the public outcry from those who wanted the original prevailed and, within 77 days, Coca-Cola announced that the original formula would return.

The company reintroduced its original drink on July 10, 1985 calling it "Coca-Cola Classic." The two drinks were sold side by side under the names "Coke II" and "Coca-Cola Classic."

By the end of the year, Coca-Cola Classic outsold both New Coke and Pepsi. Six months after the roll out of Coke Classic, Coca-Cola's sales increased at more than twice the rate of Pepsi's, putting the company back into the number one position that it has enjoyed ever since.

By the mid nineties, New Coke was pretty much banished to the corners of supermarket shelves, and today it can only be found in a few countries in the world.

Why did the public reject the new and improved brand? The improvement was not noticeable enough. It didn't taste any better for the majority of people. Coke Classic won out simply because most Coke drinkers could not accept the so-called improvements of the original formula that the New Coke contained.

The bottom line is that some things need no improvement. Our doctrine is one of them—it is forever settled in heaven.

Salvation through Jesus Christ was perfected at Calvary and nothing, or no one, can make it better than it already is.

What happened at the Coca-Cola Company is something to which we can relate. It happens more often than it should in our churches. People think they can find something better in the world, only to learn that the pleasure of sin is only for a season. When they fall on their face, they return to the old "Classic" way of the Bible. Repentant, they pray through at the altar and the Holy Ghost renews them. Much like the Coca-Cola Corporation discovered, in some instances old is better than new.

A Time of Renewal

Remember the first time you came to the Lord? As the Scriptures teach, you were born again and the Lord started a new work in you. You buried the old man and all of his faults and failures in baptism and ascended walking in newness of life.

Romans 6:4

> 4 Therefore we are buried with him by baptism into death: that like as Christ was raised up from the dead by the glory of the Father, **even so we also should walk in newness of life.**

2 Corinthians 5:17

> 17 Therefore if any man be in Christ, **he is a new creature: old things are passed away; behold, all things are become new.**

Your new birth was a fresh start for you and it created an excitement and a momentum on that day that still moves you forward as a disciple of the Lord. Of course, you still experience bad days when the enemy pushes you back a few steps. We all do. Yet, on those days your mind recounts that special day when you received the Holy Ghost for the very first time, and it creates a stirring within. Often it brings you back to your knees in repentance to the Lord.

Even though these moments cannot compare to the first time, they serve as a time of renewal to gain your footing in your walk with God. If the enemy pushes you two steps back, take three steps forward to maintain the momentum in your personal walk.

David failed big time—he committed adultery, then murder. Afterward, David pleaded for God to renew a right spirit within him and he prayed for God to restore the joy of his salvation.

Psalm 51:10-13

> 10 Create in me a clean heart, O God; **and renew a right spirit within me.**
>
> 11 Cast me not away from thy presence; and take not thy holy spirit from me.
>
> 12 **Restore unto me the joy of thy salvation;** and uphold me with thy free spirit.
>
> 13 **Then will I teach transgressors thy ways; and sinners shall be converted unto thee.**

Notice verse 13, it wasn't until God renewed and restored David's joy and salvation that he was able to continue doing the work of the Lord.

Often we look for a brand new start in the wrong places; yet the right place is always at the cross of Christ. Our restoration is as simple as kneeling before God in repentance, asking Him to renew a right spirit within. When we do, our spiritual momentum returns and again sinners are led to the truth through our ministries.

Out With the Old and In With the New

Nothing substitutes the tried and true doctrine of the Word of God. However, we should not fear or shun the "new and improved" programs or ideas in other areas of our life or ministry. In fact, it is something that we need to consider and discuss with our leaders on a continual basis.

Jesus was unafraid to do new things. He caused an uproar when He healed people on the Sabbath day, ate with publicans and when He forgave sin. And folks followed Him. His acts and words created momentum for the first century church. Many of the 3,000 souls that were added to the church on the day of Pentecost were first impacted, not by Peter's message, but by Jesus doing a new thing a few years previously. Jesus revealed some of the flaws in the old laws to His followers and to those that opposed Him. He informed them that the old laws were not going to work forever—there was a new and better way.

When Jesus came on the scene in the New Testament, it was for one reason—He would repeal the old and establish the new! At His death on Calvary, the Old Testament system of sacrificing animals for man's sin was banished forever, and the blood of Jesus became the sacrifice for all of mankind.

The Old Testament was God's old will and it pointed the way

to the New Testament, or the new will of God. Jesus Christ introduced God's new will. He put on a robe of flesh and came to dwell with man. He showed us that it is possible to live above sin. He showed us that we could all love our neighbors. He showed us the greatest love of all...the love that causes a man to lay down His life for a friend.

The new will or New Testament is successful today because it is a huge improvement over the old. Not just a slight improvement, but an overhaul.

Consider the differences between the two:

- In the old will, the law identified the sinful nature of man.
    - o In the new will, God's grace covered the sin of man.
- In the old will, only the High priest could enter the Holy of Holies on behalf of man once a year.
    - o In the new will, every person has access to the Holy of Holies through the blood of Christ, at any time.
- In the old will, man's sins were pushed forward for one year.
    - o In the new will, man's sins are cast into the sea to be forgotten in baptism, forever remitted.
- In the old will, God's spirit dwelled in the Tabernacle or in the Temple.
    - o In the new will, man became the Temple of the Holy Ghost, and now God's Spirit dwells in us.

God's New and Living Way

Hebrews 10:16-20

> 16 This is the covenant that I will make with them after those days, saith the Lord, I will put my laws into their hearts, and in their minds will I write them;
>
> 17 And their sins and iniquities will I remember no more.
>
> 18 Now where remission of these is, there is no more offering for sin.
>
> 19 Having therefore, brethren, boldness to enter into the holiest by the blood of Jesus,
>
> 20 **By a new and living way,** which he hath consecrated for us, through the veil, that is to say, his flesh;

This new and living way created so much excitement in Israel that 3,000 people were saved in one day, then 5,000 more a little while later. In fact, we are still experiencing the momentum that started during the life of Christ some 2,000 years ago.

New is not something to fear or shun; it is a concept that we find in the Bible repeatedly. Some things must never change, such as our doctrine. Conversely, some areas of ministry benefit from new ideas and will actually kick-start the momentum needed to draw in people.

However, as numbers increase, don't be fooled. Our "new and improved" must stand the test of time. Initially, folks will visit the church out of a sense of curiosity, but what motivates them to return is the reality that the new truly is an improvement over the old. We can call our changes new and improved to draw folks in, but unless they see a difference, they won't return.

For instance: Some churches rename their place of worship to show the community that they are new or newly-organized. People will come to see the changes, but if they fail to notice a difference between what the church was and what it is now, they will lose interest and stop coming. Call it what you want, but if it's not any better than before, it's the same.

An Example — Chrysler New and Improved

In the late 1970s, Chrysler Corporation was a company that was on the verge of bankruptcy. The company literally had one foot in the grave and the other on thin ice. Two of Chrysler's products—the Dodge Aspen and the Plymouth Volare—had several recalls. This cost the company millions of dollars.

Meanwhile at a rival corporation, a man named Lee Iacocca had just been named the president of Ford Motor Company. Ford enjoyed unprecedented success under the leadership of Iacocca. He was responsible for the success of the Ford Mustang, and the Lincoln Continental Mark III. He revived the Mercury brand in the late 1960s with the introduction of the Mercury Cougar and Marquis. However, Iacocca and Henry Ford II didn't get along; so in 1978, Ford fired Iacocca despite the company posting a $2 billion profit that year.

Ford's loss was Chrysler's gain. A little while later, Iacocca joined Chrysler and rebuilt the company from the ground up. Among other things, that included eliminating the old. Immediately, Iacocca laid off workers, axed unsuccessful products, and sold losing divisions of the company such as Chrysler-Europe.

Even though Iacocca was able to cut many of the losses, he realized that the company would soon go out of business if it did not receive a significant amount of money to turn it around. In 1979, Iacocca approached the United States Congress for a loan guarantee. Most people thought this was an unprecedented approach, but Iacocca pointed to the bailouts of the airline and railroad industries, arguing that more jobs were at stake if Chrysler went under. In the end, Iacocca received the guarantee from the government.

After receiving this reprieve, Chrysler released the first of the K-car Line, the Dodge Aries, and the Plymouth Reliant in 1981. Iacocca introduced Chrysler to the newly-designed K-car. Originally, the cars were small to mid-sized with seating up to six people. They were front wheel drive and had a small 2.2 liter Mitsubishi engine. The K-cars were also surprisingly quick for their size; the manual transmission version was one of the fastest in its class. The six-passenger model was the most fuel efficient and, since these cars were built during the recession, they were priced economically. These vehicles first rolled off the assembly line in 1981 and sold rapidly. The K-car quickly turned the company around; the negative momentum stopped, and the positive momentum began.

(Dave's thoughts)

I first received my driver's license in 1982. My father's 1981 red Plymouth Reliant was one of the first cars I ever drove, and I have to say I thought it was a pretty cool car in its day. My brother, who had received his driver's license two years previously, also drove this car periodically. That Plymouth Reliant was put through a pretty intense testing period!

Creating Momentum: A New Thing

On one occasion, my brother Jim, drove it off a highway ramp at 70 miles per hour. Regrettably, I happened to be in the car at the time. When the car sailed off the ramp, it hit a slope and flew airborne right over the on-ramp landing into a marshy field on the other side.

After my friend and I voiced a few choice words to Jim, we left him and begun the long trek home. We figured Jim would have to call a tow truck and explain the whole thing to Dad; in fact, we relished the moment he would have to explain what happened. After all, he had nearly killed us!

To our surprise about a half hour later, Jim drove up alongside us in the Red Plymouth Reliant. We looked at the car and we couldn't even tell that it had been in a wreck. We were shocked. We got inside and to our surprise it drove as well as it did before. Except for a slightly bent frame, the car showed no other damage. Obviously the frame of this car was designed right. You could not destroy this car; we tried our best. And guess what? Dad never found out that his new K-car had been in a high-speed wreck until years later.

Lee Iacocca was right when he said, "If you can find a better car, buy it." This slogan became Iacocca's trademark. He would use it often during an ad campaign they called, "The pride is back." Chrysler was on its way back to profitability!

Over the course of the next few years, Iacocca and his team made slight improvements and design changes to the original K-cars, producing other cars from the original K-platform such as, the LeBaron, the Spirit R/T Sedan, the exotic two-seated TC by Maserati, and even the Chrysler Town and Country, to name a few.

Chrysler's momentum increased. The K-car led to the design of the minivan. A fellow by the name of Hal Sperlich, who also left Ford a few years earlier, was there when Iacocca arrived. Sperlich was the driving force behind the Mini-Max project at Ford —a project in which Henry Ford would have no part. This venture eventually bore fruit in 1983 with the introduction of the wildly popular Dodge Caravan and Plymouth Voyager.

The era of the minivan was born in America because Lee Iacocca and Hal Sperlich were willing to start over with something entirely fresh—a brand new vehicle different from anything America had ever seen. It was a huge improvement over what was available at the time. Yes, it cost them their jobs but it paid off in the end. Chrysler's minivans led the industry in sales for twenty-five straight years. The minivan is still popular today because it is the best choice for families with young children.

Iacocca was also responsible for Chrysler's acquisition of AMC in 1987. This brought the very profitable Jeep division under Chrysler's corporate umbrella. Added to the original Jeep series was the Grand Cherokee line of Jeeps which were also popular, and still are to this day.

New or Improved?

Which one is better for you?

Iacocca understood what it took to improve and produce a new product. However, there is a huge difference between improving and producing. Both will create momentum in your ministry, but you must know which method to use before you begin. So what's the difference between the two?

- **Improved:** When you improve on something, you retain portions of the old and amend it from there.

- **New:** In order to start something new you must first abandon the old and start fresh. That's difficult. One of the greatest hindrances to starting new is letting go of the old. You have to be willing to release the old ideas and methods that you always depended on, or that may have even brought you success. That takes a very strong leader.

Iacocca was willing to make permanent changes from the very beginning of his tenure at Chrysler. Dismissing workers is a hard thing to do and firing management is even harder. But Iacocca possessed the leadership qualities needed to get the job done. Similarly, as ministers we need the strength and godly confidence to lead our churches forward.

If you really desire to create momentum in your life, your church, or your ministry, you must be willing to admit your mistakes, make tough decisions and even stand alone for a time. Then you must follow through with what you started, surrounding yourself with strong leaders who will uphold and support your choices.

CHAPTER FIVE

Maintaining Momentum

Maintaining momentum is difficult. Of all the concepts Dave and I have shared in this book, staying on course on the road to success is, by far, the most critical and difficult process.

As we have stated before, God desires for us to achieve success in His kingdom. And if we stay in His will and obey His Word, He will always work in, through and for us. There is no greater blessing than having God on our side.

Throughout Scripture we read: "If God be for us, who can be against us?" and "Greater is He that is in you than he that is in the world." Often, we interpret these passages as God fighting our battles for us. We reason that if God wants something to happen, it will happen; if not, He didn't intend it in the first place. However, this premise is incorrect. The Bible states that "Faith without works is dead." God always honors His Word, but oftentimes God's Word is conditional on man doing his part. Our active participation in the work of God's kingdom is vital…and mandatory.

Man is God's method to reach this world. To each individual, He imparts talents, skills, and abilities that enable us to create momentum in God's Church. But it is up to us to hone, sharpen, and utilize our talents in ways that benefit the kingdom of God. Along the way, we learn from our experiences, and the experiences of others, on our journey to eternity with Christ.

It is easy to start an undertaking, have some degree of success or even great success, and then allow it to dwindle to nothing. It happens frequently in structured organizations. Large corporations and Fortune 500 companies have the resources in place to identify and evaluate their company's successes and failures. Trained experts assess, identify and improve their corporation's products. However, our churches are not set up the same way, and a failure in an organization like a church can result in catastrophe.

During the planning stages of any new venture, a strategy for maintaining momentum should be discussed from the onset. In fact, churches should devote the same amount of time and effort into a plan for maintaining momentum as they do in the development of the project. Maintaining momentum is essential to growing a successful church. It is God's nature and design to create and sustain that momentum, though man often derails that plan.

Sadly, lost momentum rarely affects many churches unless they experience financial loss. As long as they are paying the bills, they are comfortable. Do you think that kind of apathy pleases God? The Church must keep moving, growing, and reaching the lost of this world, otherwise she ceases to do God's will!

In Chapter 4 we discussed improvement as a method of *creating* momentum and how the improvement must be a noticeable one. But improving your product will also help *maintain* momentum. A word of caution: As you strive to improve a project or undertaking, resist the trap that says bigger is always better—especially in ministry. Leaders and pastors mistakenly think that more and bigger ministries are a sign of success. However, adding "more" isn't always an improvement.

Simplify and Stick to the Basics

One or two great ideas are better than a myriad of mediocre ones. At times, you will have to streamline or simplify an ongoing project. Returning to the basics of what it is that got you to where you are, is a good way to start the streamlining process.

(Dave's thoughts)

One of my passions is playing golf, however, I am extremely competitive and I desire to play well. As all golfers know, this can be an unrealistic expectation if you don't have the time to practice as you should. When I start to play poorly I remind myself, "Keep your head down, and keep your eye on the ball all the way through your swing!"

That simple reminder is enough to turn around my game. Later, I again refer to a book called, "The Five Fundamentals of Golf" written by Ben Hogan. Just a brief review of each fundamental helps me to remember what brought me success in the past. As I read, I can sense what my swing felt like on those successful days and it brings me back on track. I play golf well when the basic fundamentals become second nature to me. Only then am I able to keep that momentum going.

I certainly can improve on a lot more than five things in my golf game, but I can't think of every element each time I set up to swing the club. It's just too much. But I can remember five and when I take care of those five basics, the rest of the game falls into place! I call that simplification.

Simplifying is a vital element in maintaining momentum.

One of the things that I've learned as a pastor is that less, in many cases, is more. When our church decided to go to one service instead of two each Sunday, my heart was torn. I questioned if I was making the right decision. I was accustomed to two or three Sunday services my entire life, and I feared losing some of the people who attended Sunday nights. I was concerned that our leaders and teachers wouldn't have a Sunday service to attend since they typically taught classes in the morning and came to the Sunday evening service. Yet, once we ironed out all of the details and started having one great Sunday service—instead of two or three mediocre ones—we discovered that our church grew much faster than in the past. More new people attended. Sinners were saved. Backsliders returned to God. Testimonies of God's provision and healing were voiced much more often. Families and friends had more time to grow with one another in unity. There was a spirit of expectancy in our services that had not been there in a long time.

Why? Because we were willing to simplify! We didn't make the changes out of laziness; in fact, we are still going from 7 a.m. until 3 p.m. every Sunday.

Instead, we focus all of our prayer, energy, and talents into one great and powerful service. The Lord has honored and anointed our *efforts and has blessed our church ever since. Now, a few years later, we can't believe that we actually had three services in one day. The momentum in our church grew as we simplified our Sundays. As leaders, we need to focus on simplification.*

Recognize Why You are Having Success!

Maintaining consistent momentum is the ideal. Momentum can get too strong and out of control, and it can also get too weak. We need to understand why we are experiencing momentum or the lack of it. Andy Stanley, senior pastor and founder of North Point Ministries said, "If you don't know why you have been experiencing momentum, you are just one stupid decision away from losing it." How true! Sometimes we blindly stumble into success. If and when that happens, we need to discover and define what it was that got us there.

Some people say, "God is blessing our church, and it has nothing to do with me." That may or may not be true. If God is blessing you or your church it is only because you are doing something right according to His Word. Identify what it is you are doing right, write it down, and keep it up.

Evaluation

This is called **evaluation**. We cannot overemphasize the importance of evaluation in the process of maintaining momentum. Every church needs to have monthly evaluation meetings. If you fail to evaluate your areas of success, then the success you are enjoying might be short lived.

Whether we know it or not, everyone evaluates their actions and their lives. We evaluate what causes success and failure. Instinctively, we want to succeed at what we do. Evaluation is as natural as birth; it starts as soon as a child begins to reason.

(Dave's thoughts)

Whenever I search for truth in my life, I think back to my childhood or I think about my young sons who are in their childhood years right now.

My boys and I are fortunate to have a good friend who owns a fishing pond. The pond is stocked with literally thousands of fish... bluegill, catfish, and largemouth bass. Recently, he invited us to go fishing after church one Sunday.

That day just happened to be my oldest son's birthday. When we got to their property we were surprised that our friend had purchased fishing poles and fishing tackle for my boys and me. Each tackle box contained a few different "Rapala" lures, jitter-bug lures, flies, bobbers, sinkers, hooks, rubber worms, and even a set of fishing pliers. My friend purchased everything we would ever need to fish in his pond. My boys were thrilled! The Star Wars Lego sets my wife and I bought them now took a back seat to fishing equipment....tackle, lures, line...they were excited about anything to do with fishing.

After dinner, we headed to the pond to set up our lines and hopefully catch a few fish. As soon as the boys got to the pond they opened their tackle boxes and tried to decide which fishing lure to use. Both of their boxes contained the exact same lures, but they each decided to use different ones.

My older son, Davis, decided to try the Rapala minnow first. He dropped his line in the water and instantly caught a nice-sized largemouth bass. My 7-year-old son, Barrett, still had his line out of water as I attached a lure. Well…guess what happened? Barrett pulled out the Rapala minnow—the one just like his big brother's— and said, "Daddy can you put this on my line?" By now, I had already secured the other lure, but I knew he wouldn't take no for an answer. Instinctively, Barrett knew that if the Rapala lure worked for his brother, it would work for him, too!

Barrett evaluated the situation without realizing it. Had I asked him what evaluation meant at the time, he wouldn't have even understood the word. Yet he has no problem understanding the process and, whether he knows it or not, he evaluates all the time.

Your kids are no different. It is a natural thing to do. Why do they do it? Because they want to succeed in whatever they do!

Identify and Correct

Let's take this a step further. Not only do kids evaluate, but they process the information they have learned from their evaluation and they identify any problems that might be involved. My son, Barrett, immediately identified the problem; namely, he had the wrong lure. Still, he didn't stop at identifying the problem. He took immediate corrective action as a result of his evaluation. He decided to use the lure that he thought was guaranteed to catch him a bass. And by the way, he caught one about ten minutes later.

It sounds so simple doesn't it? Evaluate, identify, and correct. The remainder of that day was a lesson for me. I watched as my boys caught bluegill, bass, and catfish all afternoon. It was a competition...they kept track of how many fish they caught and how big they were. They mentally noted the locations where the fish were biting best. Somehow they even learned, without me telling them, that the bass were the most sought after fish in the pond. More importantly, they understood what lures caught the most fish and, more specifically, the most bass.

All day long they evaluated taking corrective actions along the way. They changed their lures and their locations according to the successes and failures of each other.

For my kids, evaluation had a purpose...that purpose was to catch bass. Our purpose of evaluation is to help us maintain momentum. But evaluation is useless if we fail to take corrective action. My kids instinctively know this, but for some strange reason adults seem oblivious to this part of the process, or we just choose to ignore it for fear of offending someone. It is so easy for us to stand back and not "rock the boat," or just leave things status quo.

The truth is everyone is good at evaluation. For instance, most of us enjoy taking a moment to relax at the mall and evaluate people. Some of us can sit back and watch people mess up all day long. Similarly, people will evaluate your leadership ability from their vantage point, then return home to discuss their opinions with spouses and friends. They'll detail exactly what you did wrong and even come up with solutions as they see it. There is a word for that—criticism. Criticism is actually a type of evaluation, yet people seldom use their criticism in a positive manner. Most of those people would never think of coming to you to suggest a better way.

CONSTRUCTIVE CRITICISM

Don't allow criticism to defeat you; instead, use criticism in a positive manner. As leaders, we have the opportunity to channel criticism in the right direction. When we do, disapproval turns into a credible evaluation tool; namely, constructive criticism.

There are a number of ways to do this: Suggestion boxes in your church, panel discussions in your ministry, or interactive Internet discussions. All of these are useful ways to channel the evaluation process in a positive direction.

Once you have had those discussions, suggestions, and meetings, corrective action is the next step. People want and expect you to make some hard decisions. They need and want a decisive leader. This is where true leaders shine! A good leader will always learn something from an evaluation meeting. A great leader identifies the problem and is ready and willing to take corrective action, even at the cost of hurting someone's feelings in the process. No one is exempt from corrective action.

Evaluation should always focus on improving the effort. Continuous evaluation improvement will always maintain, and very often increase, the momentum of any given effort.

Our call to reach this world for Christ is too important to let things slide. We don't have time for that; souls are hanging in the balance. God never held back in this area, He took corrective action whenever needed and we ought to do the same. That is what great leaders do.

One of the reasons that God gave us His Word, was to equip us to evaluate our lives according to His plan. A few months ago, a minister in our church candidly came to me (Jim) for the purpose of accountability and submission to authority in his life. He asked me to be honest with him and to feel free to evaluate his life and his ministry. He had an earnest desire to grow in ministry and I appreciated his sincerity. I will never forget how he phrased it. He asked me to always be up front and honest with him and to show him "the things that he needed to keep doing, the things that he needed to stop doing, and the things that he needed to start doing."

When he left that day, I was convicted because I failed to evaluate my own life or ministry in that manner for some time. So I proceeded to take inventory of my life and found there were some things that I needed to start doing, some things I needed to stop doing, and some things that I needed to keep doing.

When we read the Scripture, it is like taking an inventory of our lives. The Word of God is always true, it never lies, and we can evaluate our lives in the light of God's unchanging Word.

James admonished the early church saying…

James 1:22-25

> 22 But be ye doers of the word, and not hearers only, deceiving your own selves.
>
> 23 For if any be a hearer of the word, and not a doer, **he is like unto a man beholding his natural face in a glass:**
>
> 24 For he beholdeth himself, and goeth his way, and straightway **forgetteth what manner of man he was.**
>
> 25 But **whoso looketh into the perfect law of liberty, and continueth therein,** he being not a forgetful hearer, **but a doer of the work, this man shall be blessed in his deed.**

As we look into the perfect law—the Word of God—we are looking into a mirror.

Do you remember those days when you were young, *really young*, when you loved to look at your reflection in the mirror?

You would comb your hair, shave, brush your teeth, and groom anything that was out of place. Then you would step back and admire your attractiveness. What were you doing? You were evaluating yourself.

The mirror was honest; it did not lie. The mirror told the truth every time. It wasn't the same as asking your spouse if you looked good. That, by the way, seldom results in an honest answer! The mirror revealed exactly how you looked. After a few moments of evaluation in front of the mirror, you could identify any imperfections and take corrective actions as needed.

James noted that after we step away from God's Word we forget what manner of person we are. Why? Because life gets in the way, things happen, and before long we have forgotten our "mirror's" reflection and take no corrective actions. We become a hearer rather than a doer of the Word. James stated that when we look into the perfect law—the mirror of God's Word—we must not forget what it says (the evaluation). And if we become a doer of the Word (corrective action), we will be blessed in life and in deed.

God's Word is the ultimate evaluation tool for every individual. Whether you are a leader, a pastor, or a saint, you must look into the mirror of the Scriptures every day if you want to maintain the momentum in your spiritual walk.

His Word reveals the things that we need to keep doing, the things we need to stop doing, and the things that we need to start doing.

2 Timothy 3:15-17

> 15 And that from a child thou hast known the holy scriptures, which are able to make thee wise unto salvation through faith which is in Christ Jesus.

> 16 All scripture is given by inspiration of God, and is profitable for doctrine, **for reproof, for correction, for instruction in righteousness:**
>
> 17 That **the man of God may be perfect,** thoroughly furnished unto all good works.

Paul told Timothy that the Scriptures were given to us so that we could assess our lives in light of God's plan for mankind. Paul stated that God's Word is profitable for reproof (stop doing), for correction (start doing), and for instruction (keep doing). Each one of these elements is part of the evaluation process. Paul said that if we use the Scripture in this manner it will lead us to perfection and good works. But if we can't face our faults and failures and make corrections in our lives and ministries, we will never reach the place that God intends for us to reach…a place of perfection in Christ.

On the road to perfection we will encounter many bumps and snares. At times, failure is in the hands of the leaders; other times it is the follower's fault. Because we are human, we can't maintain all of the momentum all of the time. Sometimes we invest in the wrong person, idea or program. That happens and is to be expected. It is why leaders must take the time and effort to evaluate as much as possible. We must comprehend why we are succeeding or failing.

The Parable of the Sower illustrates this.

Matthew 13:3-8

> 3 And he spake many things unto them in parables, saying, Behold, a sower went forth to sow;
>
> 4 And when he sowed, some seeds fell by the way side, and the fowls came and devoured them up:

> 5 Some fell upon stony places, where they had not much earth: and forthwith they sprung up, because they had no deepness of earth:
>
> 6 And when the sun was up, they were scorched; and because they had no root, they withered away.
>
> 7 And some fell among thorns; and the thorns sprung up, and choked them:
>
> 8 **But other fell into good ground, and brought forth fruit, some a hundredfold, some sixtyfold, some thirtyfold.**

Occasionally, you will sow a seed in bad ground. For instance, you'll have a great new idea but place the wrong person in charge of it. Or you might have a person with loads of talent whom you want to use, but you assign him to the wrong position or ministry. Both of these scenarios fail because the soil is unprepared and overgrown with weeds.

Jesus addressed the remedy to this situation later in the same chapter...

Matthew 13:23

> 23 But he that received seed into the good ground **is he that heareth the word, and understandeth it;** which also beareth fruit, and bringeth forth, some an hundredfold, some sixty, some thirty.

Jesus taught the process of evaluation in this parable: When we hear and understand the Word, we will recognize good ground and proceed to sow in fertile soil!

Repeatedly in Scripture, Jesus taught that we must invest our seeds and talents wisely. If we apply the wisdom and understanding of the Word we will sow with godly perception, unafraid to take corrective action whenever necessary.

A final reminder: Don't concern yourself about how much fruit your investment will bring. Just concentrate on being a wise sower. When you do, you will maintain momentum and as a result, your ministry will bear fruit.

CHAPTER SIX

When the Enemy Stops Your Momentum

One of the most popular tactics coaches use to win a game is to try and stop their opponent's momentum. This is done in a variety of ways. The most common is to call a time out when the opponent is on a roll. We see this frequently in basketball when a team is on a scoring run. With the momentum going their way, the opposing coach jumps from behind the bench to call a time out. Doing so stops the winning team's momentum.

Similarly, in baseball when a pitcher is getting "rocked," the manager often approaches the mound to try and calm down the pitcher and stop the momentum of the team that is up to bat.

POSITIVE MOMENTUM TAKES WORK

Positive momentum is extremely valuable but it doesn't come cheap or easy. It takes sacrifice, work, and oftentimes tremendous amounts of energy to cause positive momentum in the kingdom of God. We fight the devil on every side to accomplish what God has called us to do.

If you've been around the church for any length of time, you've seen the incredible amount of time, energy and money it takes to expand God's kingdom. These resources are not our own, they are God's. Just as the loss of momentum upsets us, the Holy Spirit is also grieved; undoubtedly, more than we know. Although we may have lost time and money, Jesus endured the cross for us to have victory and revival in our lives, churches and cities.

Fight Spiritual Warfare Through Prayer and Unity

When the enemy stops our momentum, it does no good to fight people because the war is a spiritual one. The Bible explains that we wrestle not against flesh and blood, but against principalities and powers and rulers of darkness. Consequently, another church board meeting will not fix the situation; however, a church prayer meeting can accomplish an incredible amount and turn the tables on an otherwise bad situation.

When the enemy stops momentum it is often life-shattering. We would be remiss to not recognize the fact that some people have invested their entire lives in the church. Their hopes, dreams, and ambitions are for the church to move forward; however, when the unexpected happens or the undesired occurs and the church is thrown into a chaotic state, it is time for those good people to hang on, get on their knees and petition heaven for God's help. It's time to fight spiritual warfare.

How great it would be if the only thing our churches had to wrestle were devils. We could have a Spirit-filled prayer meeting and take care of the whole problem. Oftentimes, the biggest obstacles and hindrances in the church are some of the people who attend it. Personal agendas and generational domains are just a couple of the plagues that stop momentum. It is amazing how a few people can ruin a good thing for everyone else. Ninety percent of the church might rally to move forward ready for a move of God, while the other 10 percent grumble and complain, looking for a reason to create a problem. As a result, the possibility of revival diminishes.

Discord in the church is worse than any devil. However, unity and brotherly love can conquer all obstacles. On the day of Pentecost, the believers were all in one accord in one place. These people put aside their own agendas long enough to come together in a spirit of unity and worship. That got God's attention and kindled a spiritual outpouring of the Holy Ghost. The whole place was filled with God's spirit and no one was left out.

But what if a few people had sat in a corner grumbling and complaining about the church, instead of uniting in prayer, expecting God to move? The outcome might have been much different.

When the enemy steals our momentum, it's time for the church to rally behind its leadership. It's time for us to unite and pray for our pastor and ministers like never before. This is the time for true saints of God to really shine in the midst of adversity. There is no room for personality conflicts; we must come together in a united front to combat evil forces. When we do, momentum is regained.

Have you ever noticed that when a cue ball is shot at another ball on a billiards table, the momentum of the first ball is carried to the second ball upon impact? The second ball only slows by gravity. In the same manner, when the enemy steals the church's virtue, the church must respond with the power of the Holy Ghost to gain the momentum lost.

Stand and Do What's Right

It's always right to do right. Throughout history, right motives and attitudes have turned pending disasters into glorious victories. The Bible is filled with stories of how God moved in favor of those who stood in the face of danger for the cause of righteousness and right living.

Shammah stood in a field of lintels and defended it against the troops of the marauder Philistines. The young David also stood alone in a valley with a meager weapon in hand as he faced a militant giant, all because his heart told him it was the right thing to do.

When the Holy Spirit tells you to stand, stand. Don't allow lost momentum to stop the work of God or hinder your determination to experience growth. You may take three steps forward and two steps back, but you've gained one step. It may be an uphill battle, but keep fighting.

Jonathan and his armor bearer knew full well what an uphill battle was on the day God fought for them. If the battle is easy God often stays uninvolved, but He rallies to our aid when the Church is on her knees, backed against a wall.

You don't have to be a pastor, head deacon or church board member to have an impact on a church. You do, however, have to be prayed up and willing to face whenever the enemy attacks the work of God in your city. Your spirit has to be right and your motives must be pure.

When David lost his momentum, it didn't return until God renewed his spirit and cleansed his heart. That is why we need the renewing of the Holy Ghost continually in our lives.

Psalm 51:10-13

> 10 **Create in me a clean heart,** O God; and **renew a right spirit** within me.
>
> 11 Cast me not away from thy presence; and take not thy holy spirit from me.
>
> 12 Restore unto me the joy of thy salvation; and uphold me with thy free spirit.
>
> 13 **Then will I teach transgressors thy ways; and sinners shall be converted unto thee.**

In Conclusion

What do you do when the enemy has stolen your momentum? Get it back! Resist discouragement and the tendency to grumble, complain and engage in pity-parties. Take hold of the Word of God and the horns of the altar and plead for the power of the Holy Spirit to move mightily on behalf of your church.

Remember, though the enemy is like a roaring lion, seeking whom (*and what ministries!*) he can devour; the "lion" has no teeth. God removed them at Calvary.

1 Peter 5:8-9

> 8 Be sober, be vigilant; because your adversary the devil, as a roaring lion, walketh about, seeking whom he may devour:
>
> 9 Whom resist steadfast in the faith…

CHAPTER SEVEN

How Timing Affects Momentum

Have you ever been "in the zone"? You know, when everything lines up just right? When momentum is on your side? When everything times perfectly and you hit the mark, or when you are in exactly the right place at exactly the right time?

Most of us have been "in the zone" at one time or another, yet if we are honest, it doesn't happen too often. As much as we would love to discover the zone more frequently, finding it doesn't happen by accident. Consequently, it is essential to understand and implement all of the elements needed to get there.

Jesus desires for each of us to find our zone or place of perfection.

Ephesians 4:13

> 13 Till we all come in the unity of the faith, and of the knowledge of the Son of God, **unto a perfect man, unto the measure of the stature of the fullness of Christ:**

In order to break into the zone, we must have a keen understanding of timing and its importance. Timing is an element that can cause us to take advantage of momentum or to lose momentum and, at the same time, it is critical in maintaining momentum.

(Dave's thoughts)

I have always admired and been secretly jealous of surfers. I tried surfing a few times and the thing I struggle with most is trying to time the wave just right. I have managed to catch a few waves in my life and each time I did, I momentarily had the feeling of being in the zone. But more often than not, the surf pummeled me, pinning my body against the ocean floor until the surf finally released its death grip. That feeling is one of the worst I have had in my life.

Surfers demonstrate a keen sense of timing in their sport. Catching the forward momentum of a wave is all about perfect timing. You must be in the exact right place at the exact right time.

Doctors say that professional surfers are able to slow their minds in the surf's high-pressure environment. Moments that pass in flashes of blinding speed for the average person, are slowed down to frame-by-frame slow motion shots for these skilled athletes. Medical studies have shown that their minds become ultra clear and sensitive to split-second timing. Instead of rushing into a wave too early, they calmly wait for the right moment to catch the momentum of the wave. If their timing is a tad late, they might miss their opportunity for the ride of their life. If their timing is too early, their bodies might slam into razor-sharp coral.

When their timing is just right and they catch the forward momentum of the surf, they merge into perfect harmony with their board and the wave. Potential energy is realized and the surfer becomes part of the ocean. He can ride it high, he can ride it low, he can go fast, or he can slow it down and ride through the tube. The surfer is "in the zone." He can travel a mile out in the ocean, and moments later land on the beach because he has rode the momentum of that wave all the way to shore.

Jesus was "in the zone" more than anyone else in Scripture. Granted, He had the advantage of being God in the flesh, but we can look to Him as the greatest example of how timing relates to momentum.

When Satan tempted Jesus, he picked a bad time. Jesus had just completed a 40-day fast; He was hungry, weak, and thirsty. It appeared like the perfect time to tempt Jesus with bread, yet it was actually the perfect time for Jesus to resist the devil. Forty days of prayer and fasting had built up a positive spiritual momentum in Jesus that a few fleshly temptations could not derail.

Matthew 4:2-4

> 2 And **when he had fasted forty days and forty nights,** he was afterward ahungered.
>
> 3 And **when the tempter came to him, he said, If thou be the Son of God, command that these stones be made bread.**
>
> 4 But he answered and said, It is written, **Man shall not live by bread alone,** but by every word that proceedeth out of the mouth of God.

Since Jesus was "in the zone," there was no way that Satan's efforts could succeed. Satan tempted Jesus three different times in every area a man could be tempted: the lust of the flesh, the eyes, and pride. But the momentum Jesus experienced from His extended period of fasting, terminated Satan's attempts.

In the same way, when we are attuned to God we are aware of His timing in our ministries and in our lives. The Bible says, "He that hath an ear, let him hear what the Spirit says to the church." The Holy Spirit led Jesus into the wilderness to fast and pray. Something was about to happen and He needed to prepare Himself. Similarly, through prayer and fasting we can stay in tune to God and "in the zone" of our callings.

Timing is a critical aspect in the life of every believer. Most of the things we do in life relate to timing and they occur without much thought. For instance, we know a baby must have teeth before he or she can eat meat. Our children must learn to walk before they can run or ride a bike, or learn to ice skate before they can play ice hockey. Our entire lives are built around proper timing.

The Bible says there is a time and season for everything.

Ecclesiastes 3:1

> 3 To everything there is a season, and a time to every purpose under the heaven:

As much as God is a God of momentum, He is also a God of timing. These two elements are so intertwined that we would be remiss if we failed to discuss the relationship between them.

Over the course of man's history, individuals, companies and nations have all discovered that timing is a key element of success. In battle, the perfectly timed surprise attack is fundamental to overcoming one's enemy. In the retail marketplace, the perfectly-timed release of a new product is crucial to the success or failure of it. In the corporate world, having the right personnel at the right time is essential in advancing the company to the next level.

A famous quote says, "Timing in life is everything." *When* you do and *what* you do determines success or failure in life. In our current economic crisis, investors say that it is the perfect time to buy property, a "buyer's market." The problem is most people cannot afford to buy now. Only those who have money can take advantage of this timely opportunity.

In the auto-making industry, the companies that ride out the storm are the ones who will reap huge profits a few years from now. Currently, the average age of a vehicle in America is over 9-years-old; in the nineties it was only 6 1/2-years-old. In the recent history of automobiles, our vehicles are older now than ever before.

Consequently, after the economy recovers two to three years from now, the surviving automakers will be poised and ready for a deluge of customers needing a new car. Furthermore, the demand for cars will coincide with a reduction in supply due to plant closings, fewer workers, and streamlining operations. This rare case of supply and demand will result in "perfect timing" for the few automobile companies able to stay afloat during this recession, reversing the negative momentum they experienced previously. Predictions are they will encounter unprecedented success.

THE TIMING OF THE SIX-DAY WAR

Against all odds, a people known for their nonviolence executed the most flawless military operation in the modern history of mankind. The Six-Day War of 1967 was a war won, in large part, by the perfect timing of a surprise air attack.

For many years, the neighboring Arab countries had provoked Israel with hostile actions, threats, and a series of terrorist attacks. Egypt, Syria, Jordan, and Iraq united in an all-out attempt to annihilate Israel. Egypt alone had some 100,000 soldiers deployed amongst seven divisions in the eastern parts of Sinai and the Gaza Strip. The United Nations promptly abandoned Israel, leaving the Israelis no choice but to plan their own defense.

By this time, Israeli forces had been on alert for three weeks. The country could not remain mobilized indefinitely; its sea lane was blocked and supplies were running out. Israel was on the brink of total annihilation. Backed into a corner, and facing imminent attacks from the Arab world, Israel's military commanders conceived a brilliant war strategy. They decided to preempt the expected Arab attack. To do this successfully, Israel needed the element of surprise. Had it waited for an Arab invasion, the tiny nation would have had a catastrophic disadvantage.

On the morning of June 5, 1967, Prime Minister Eshkol gave the order to attack Egypt and the entire Israeli Air Force departed at exactly 7:14 a.m. They intended to bomb Egyptian airfields while the Egyptian pilots were still eating breakfast. The attack was code-named "Operation Moked," and required exact and detailed planning to time the approaches of each force to ensure the element of surprise at the attack locations.

Their timing was impeccable. Approximately 300 Egyptian aircraft including bombers, combat planes, and helicopters, were destroyed in less than two hours, before they had a chance to launch. This perfectly planned operation eliminated the main air threat against Israel.

When Jordan entered the war, the Israeli Air Force turned to the Jordanian airfields in Amman and Mafrak, and destroyed a large part of the Jordanian Air Force. Later that day, Syrian and Iraqi forces were also eliminated. In less than one day, Israel had totally destroyed the combined air forces of Egypt, Syria, Jordan, and Iraq. It was as if the war was over before the fighting began.

Needless to say, this perfectly-timed air attack swung the momentum back in Israel's favor. In four days, Israel, with unmatched air superiority, was free to fight under clear skies while its Air Force pilots provided support from above. This enabled Israel to push through the powerful Egyptian army on three different fronts to reach the Suez Canal and the Gulf of Suez. By the fourth day of the war, the Egyptians were defeated and Israel controlled the entire Sinai Peninsula.

On other fronts, Israel quickly gained ground. Jordan captured the Government House used by UN observers, but Israel regained it and conquered Jordanian posts in eastern Jerusalem. By the third day of the war, IDF paratroopers had recaptured the Western Wall and the Temple Mount was theirs for the taking. In the mountains of Samaria, Israeli tanks captured one population center after another: Bethlehem, the Etzion block, Hebron, and the Judean hills south of Jerusalem. The Jordan resistance quickly collapsed after only three days at war with Israel.

Since Israel lacked enough troops to fight battles on every front, the battle with Syria was delayed until the forces were released from Sinai and Jerusalem. It was Israel's air superiority that kept other forces at bay. The Syrians had a series of strong fortifications along the Golan Heights. They had six infantry brigades and about two hundred tanks. On the morning of June 9—after two days of heavy Air Force bombardment—Israeli tanks moved in on the Syrians. Soon, the Syrian deployment collapsed and their forces retreated.

In six days, Israel—a nation not known for its fighting ability—defeated four superior nations who together outnumbered and outranked them. At exactly the right time and place, they were able to surprise their enemies and turn the momentum their way.

In all, Israel lost only 777 men compared to her enemies who lost approximately 18,300 men in a six-day period of time. A few wise men, who understood the importance of timing, reversed the fate of an entire nation.

Timing in Jesus' Ministry

Jesus understood the importance of timing better than anyone else and was ultra-sensitive about the timing of His ministry.

Throughout Scripture, Jesus told His family and His followers that His time had not yet come, or it was not yet His hour.

John 2:4

> 4 Jesus saith unto her, Woman, what have I to do with thee? **mine hour is not yet come.**

John 7:6

> 6 Then Jesus said unto them, **My time is not yet come:** but your time is always ready.

John 7:30

> 30 Then they sought to take him: but no man laid hands on him, because **his hour was not yet come.**

What did Jesus mean by these statements?

Jesus' "time" or "hour" of ministry was exact. To work miracles at an inappropriate time might initiate Jesus' enemies to take His life before His ministry completed. Jesus had work to do. He had to train his disciples and prepare them for what was coming after Calvary. To draw attention to Himself too early in His ministry, might stop the forward momentum His disciples needed to carry His work into the first century.

Many times, Jesus told those He had healed to tell no one of the miracle. In doing so, He averted His enemies from taking His life prematurely. The timing of His life, death, and resurrection were all critical to the forward momentum that He had instituted in His disciples throughout His ministry. Any one miracle done in the wrong place at the wrong time could well attract too much attention from the religious rulers of His day, and derail the work that He had established. Timing in the life of Christ was a crucial element to His success.

In another story where timing was critical to momentum, we find Jesus in the exact right place at the exact right time...

John 21:1-4

> 21 After these things **Jesus shewed himself again to the disciples at the sea of Tiberias**; and on this wise shewed he himself.
>
> 2 There were together Simon Peter, and Thomas called Didymus, and Nathanael of Cana in Galilee, and the sons of Zebedee, and two other of his disciples.
>
> 3 Simon Peter saith unto them, I go a fishing. They say unto him, We also go with thee. They went forth, and entered into a ship immediately; and that night they caught nothing.

4 But when the morning was now come, Jesus stood on the shore: but the disciples knew not that it was Jesus.

Peter and the disciples acted so much like we would in this situation. They tried to find purpose and meaning in what had just transpired. The fact that Peter was naked in the fishing boat tells us a little bit about his condition and state of mind. He was apathetic and didn't really care what people thought of him. His recent past clouded his judgment and he felt like a failure. A few days earlier, he denied Christ and guilt gnawed at him. He couldn't handle it anymore; he was done. The act of returning to his former occupation was Peter's way of saying: "I am going back to my old life. I have messed up. Jesus is gone, and all I have left is fishing. I'm done with following Jesus."

Negative momentum was gaining steam. Peter was the leader, the one closest to Jesus, so the disciples followed him not knowing what else to do. They decided to give up and return to their old lives. But they didn't have much luck fishing; in fact, they fished all night and caught nothing.

When the Sun rose over the Sea of Galilee the next morning, guess who stood on the shore? The Savior. Talk about perfect timing! No one but Jesus could have encouraged them at that point. He urged them to cast their nets on the other side of the boat and when they did, the net was so full that they couldn't pull it in. And in that moment Peter realized Who it was standing on the shore...

John 21:7

7 Therefore that disciple whom Jesus loved saith unto Peter, It is the Lord. **Now when Simon Peter heard that**

> it was the Lord, he girt his fisher's coat unto him, (for he was naked,) and did cast himself into the sea.

Peter immediately jumped into the sea to swim to Jesus.

John 21:15-17

> 15 So when they had dined, **Jesus saith to Simon Peter,** Simon, son of Jonas, lovest thou me more than these? He saith unto him, Yea, Lord; thou knowest that I love thee. He saith unto him, **Feed my lambs.**
>
> 16 He saith to him again the second time, Simon, son of Jonas, lovest thou me? He saith unto him, Yea, Lord; thou knowest that I love thee. He saith unto him, **Feed my sheep.**
>
> 17 He saith unto him the third time, Simon, son of Jonas, lovest thou me? Peter was grieved because he said unto him the third time, Lovest thou me? And he said unto him, Lord, thou knowest all things; thou knowest that I love thee. Jesus saith unto him, **Feed my sheep.**

Jesus prepared a fire and called the disciples to shore. After dinner, Jesus questioned Peter. He knew exactly what was on the heart and mind of the disciple. Gently, Jesus walked Peter through his guilt. Peter denied the Lord three times just days before and so—three times—Jesus asked, "Do you love Me?"

Jesus spent years teaching the disciples how to build His Church. But Jesus' focus was on Peter, not on the other disciples, because Peter was key. In just a few days, Peter would preach his first message of the Church at Pentecost. So to stop the negative momentum, the Lord sought to turn Peter around, taking him back to his denial, their 3 1/2 -year relationship, and all of the sacrifices the disciple had made to follow Jesus.

In doing so, Jesus basically said, "What are you thinking? You have come too far to turn back now. You have invested and sacrificed too much to give up on following Me."

Peter got back on track, the rest of the disciples followed him and a few days later in the Upper Room, they were filled with the Holy Ghost and with fire. Peter went on to preach the keynote message at Pentecost, and we still are experiencing the momentum that started not on the day of Pentecost, but on the day Jesus met Peter on the shores of Galilee.

Jesus stopped the negative momentum that Peter had generated, and turned it into positive, forward movement because He was at the right place at the right time. Who knows what would have happened to those seven disciples had Jesus not appeared when He did? The good news is that we don't have to wonder. Jesus did show up and He showed up right on time.

Throughout His ministry, Jesus' impeccable timing contributed to the momentum of His ministry. The story of the death of Lazarus, Jesus' good friend, is another prime example.

John 11:1-7

> 11 Now a certain man was sick, named Lazarus, of Bethany, the town of Mary and her sister Martha.
>
> 2 (It was that Mary which anointed the Lord with ointment, and wiped his feet with her hair, whose brother Lazarus was sick.)
>
> 3 Therefore his sisters sent unto him, saying, Lord, behold, he whom thou lovest is sick.
>
> 4 When Jesus heard that, he said, This sickness is not unto death, but for the glory of God, that the Son of God might be glorified thereby.
>
> 5 Now Jesus loved Martha, and her sister, and Lazarus.

> 6 When he had heard therefore that he was sick, he abode two days still in the same place where he was.
>
> 7 Then after that saith he to his disciples, Let us go into Judaea again.

In reading this text it seems that Jesus had no sense of timing at all. Actually, that is exactly what Lazarus' sisters, Mary and Martha, believed.

John 11:21-23

> 21 Then said Martha unto Jesus, Lord, if thou hadst been here, my brother had not died.
>
> 22 But I know, that even now, whatsoever thou wilt ask of God, God will give it thee.
>
> 23 Jesus saith unto her, Thy brother shall rise again.

The sisters blamed Jesus for being late and blamed Him for Lazarus' death. But Jesus assured them that He was on time, and that their brother would live again. Still, they failed to believe...

John 11:39

> 39 Jesus said, Take ye away the stone. Martha, the sister of him that was dead, saith unto him, Lord, by this time he stinketh: for he hath been dead four days.

Jesus waited for Lazarus to die so that He could perform one of His greatest miracles. The longer He waited, the greater the miracle would be. Jesus operated on a different time clock—heaven's timing—and He was about to show His disciples and the rest of the world that He had power over death.

John 11:43-45

> 43 And when he thus had spoken, he cried with a loud voice, Lazarus, come forth.
>
> 44 And he that was dead came forth, bound hand and foot with graveclothes: and his face was bound about with a napkin. Jesus saith unto them, Loose him, and let him go.
>
> 45 **Then many of the Jews which came to Mary, and had seen the things which Jesus did, believed on him.**

The Bible records that because of this miracle, many of the Jews believed on Jesus and followed Him. In fact, if the authorities of Jesus' day had not intervened, consider what potentially could have occurred…

John 11:48

> 48 If we let him thus alone, **all men will believe on him:** and the Romans shall come and take away both our place and nation.

The Pharisees and the chief priests assembled and said, "If we don't do something about Jesus, then all men will believe on Him." The miracle was so great, so powerful, that it had the potential to persuade all men to follow Jesus. Isn't that what ministry is all about? The glory of God is so present and powerful that it persuades mankind to surrender their lives to Him!

That is perfect timing! Heavenly timing! The miracle would not have been as great if Jesus had arrived earlier…but Jesus was right on time!

God had a master plan that was already in motion. All men were not persuaded because of the religious leaders of that day, and Jesus would soon sacrifice His life for mankind.

Timing is important to God—His timing. As Christians, we need to seek God's perfect timing above our own. His ways are above our ways. His plan is better than our plan. His timing is much more accurate than ours.

Just like Mary and Martha, we often wait for the Lord to answer us in the midst of life's adversities. We wonder why God is seemingly silent and fails to respond in a more timely fashion. But God allows our situations to go from bad to worse because He desires to work in us more powerfully and miraculously than ever before. Oftentimes, our trials bring more glory to God than we can imagine. As a result, our testimony wins people to the Lord. People we never expected or dreamed would come to Christ, will do so because of God's perfect timing—because His plan was bigger and better than ours!

Jesus was "in the zone" on the day He raised Lazarus from the dead and more people than Lazarus were transformed that day. It was one of Jesus' greatest miracles. When we stay in tune with God through prayer and fasting, we abide in the spiritual zone, sensitive to God's perfect timing for our lives. So strive to stay in the zone!

Building Momentum for the Altar Service

If you have never experienced a true Apostolic Church service, you are missing out on one of the greatest and most powerful experiences that you will ever encounter on this Earth. When praise and worship go up, God always comes down. He inhabits the praises of His people.

(Dave's thoughts)

I have been Apostolic all 43 years of my life, and I enjoy going to church more now than I ever did before.

Having said that, I have also witnessed too many services where the Spirit of God was quenched and the momentum of the service stopped. What could have been a life-changing experience for someone was now forever lost. As a leader and a pastor, this loss of spiritual momentum is what I fear the most. I strive to do everything I can to give people the opportunity to experience the New Birth plan of salvation during the service.

Every service should point people to the altar. With God's help, everything we do in our services should crescendo at the altar. When people kneel there, they should receive what they need from God.

THE TABERNACLE PLAN AND THE ALTAR

In the Old Testament, there was a way to approach God—it was part of the law called the tabernacle plan. Mistakenly, many Christians think that only the high priest could approach the altar; however, that's false. The priests were the only people who could enter the Holy Place and the high priest was the only one who could go beyond the veil into the Holy of Holies, but anyone could approach the brazen altar.

The Brazen Altar, located inside the gate of the tabernacle's outer court, was the first thing the Israelites saw when they entered. No one could miss it. God designed it that way because the altar was where the sacrifices were made for the atonement of sins. Every person who sinned had to go through that process.

Galatians 3:24

> 24 Wherefore the law was our schoolmaster to bring us unto Christ, that we might be justified by faith.

> THE TABERNACLE PLAN WAS PART OF THE LAW OF THE OLD TESTAMENT AND IT POINTED THE WAY TO CHRIST!

When Jesus died for us, He became our sacrifice; He became our altar. At Calvary, the veil was rent, and the old way was exchanged for the new through the blood of Jesus Christ. The altar is where we are changed from that old carnal man into a new man for Christ. It is only through what Jesus did for us at the altar that saves us from an eternity in Hell.

John 14:6
> 6 Jesus saith unto him, I am the way, the truth, and the life: no man cometh unto the Father, but by me.

What the tabernacle plan did in the Old Testament is what our church services do today. They prepare us to approach God for our needs at the altar service. No one could enter the Holy Place except they approach the altar where the sacrificial blood was offered for their sins. This teaches us that nobody will enter into heaven except they enter through the blood of Jesus Christ. He is the One who now stands as the altar of sacrifice for all of mankind.

The altar call is the most important part of any church service. No one makes it into heaven unless they experience what happens at the altar. From the moment people enter our church doors, we should point them toward the place that God has designed for repentance, regeneration, deliverance, healing and restoration. Everything we do must direct them to Calvary!

Every person must have their own altar experience and every part of our service needs to build momentum toward that.

PATTERNS OF PROTOCOL

Just as there was a protocol and some procedure in approaching God in Old Testament times, there is also some protocol in our approach to God during our services.

We are living in the dispensation of grace, and there is no plan laid out as detailed as the tabernacle plan of the Old Testament, but we can use the patterns established then for our purpose now. After all, these things were written for our admonition, and the Bible says that God never changes; His Word is forever settled in heaven.

Just as every leader's personality differs from another, their style of leadership and church format also differs. This is as it should be because different people are attracted to different leadership styles. It takes all of us to win this world for Christ. Yet, do you think there is a pattern that we could all follow that would allow God to transform as many souls as possible at our altars? We believe there is.

BUILDING MOMENTUM IN THE SERVICE

When a pastor prays before a service, he or she should ask God to prevent anything or anyone from hindering the move of His Spirit. No flesh, no pride, no sin, and no spirit. Nothing should impede the power of the Gospel changing the lives of sinners in our midst.

Our services should build faith and expectancy in the hearts of the congregation. It should be common for people to receive the Holy Spirit, healing, deliverance and restoration at our altars. That is God's purpose for the altar, and we should expect God to move in every service.

So what can we do to prepare, promote and pave the way for the Spirit of God to move and touch people's lives at our altars?

To start, we must have a place specifically designated for pre-service prayer. All ministry and worship teams should pray before every service. We are the ones who must prepare to lead others, so we should seek God to purify our hearts before the service begins.

PRAYER AND WORSHIP

Appointing one of the ministers to lead the congregation in an anointed prayer will invite God's presence. Before the prayer concludes, the worship team should start worshipping, ready to lead the congregation in praise. Remind them that praise and worship are acts of adoration toward God as well as a testimony to others. If the worship team appears not to enjoy the worship, neither will the congregation. But as they smile, clap, and praise God with uplifted arms they will lead others to do the same.

We understand that it takes time for people on the worship team to develop the discipline to do this. After all, it's hard to worship freely as the congregation watches. Human nature causes us to act differently when people are watching, but each person on the platform must realize that they have a significant role. The worship team and leaders must learn to worship in Spirit and in Truth even when all eyes are on them. Doing so will help build faith and expectancy in the hearts of others.

The Offering

We must teach our people that giving through tithes and offerings is a form of worship as well. Avoid the temptation to talk too much about giving unless it is appropriate to do so. Special offerings for missionaries or building projects can be taken at special services where people are prepared to give in this manner. Always make sure to inform your visitors that they are not obligated to give in any way. They are your guests!

Everyone on the platform is observed at all times; consequently, leaders and worship teams should give something in the offering, however small, as an example to the church. Ushers should be trained to be courteous and friendly to everyone as they take up the offering.

During the offering, the worship team should lead with an upbeat and positive song. People tend to be more cheerful with this type of music, and the Bible says that God loves a cheerful giver!

Prayer Requests, Special Music and Speaker

As the song concludes, whoever leads in prayer should be ready. Verbal requests, especially in larger churches, are not a good idea; they can quench the flow of the Spirit. Prayer requests should be made available to the ministry through prayer request forms. The ministry can have a list of immediate and important needs available at the pulpit, and the prayer leader can call for those who have needs to come and have the ministry pray for them during this time. While someone is leading the Body in prayer and as the music continues in the background, others in ministry can go and lay hands on those who have come to the altar with their special needs. Once the prayers are finished, the worship team can then move into a slow worship chorus, giving thanks to God for what He has done.

If there is a choir or a special, this is the time for it. Move right into it without much speaking. An anointed soloist or a choir can touch spirits, build faith and prepare hearts for the preaching of God's Word.

As the singing comes to a close, the speaker—or whoever introduces the speaker— should be ready to go to the pulpit. Pastors might use this time to give a pastor's welcome to any visitors or special guests. This usually gives the sound team time to cue up any type of media for the sermon, and it gives the worship team and ministry leaders time to find their seats.

The Power of Preaching God's Word

From this point on, it is all up to God and the preacher. The speaker needs to be sensitive about the type of service: Evangelistic, Bible study, or a word for the church body. Remember, you always get what you preach! If the service is evangelistic, you must preach faith and the Gospel of the kingdom of God: Jesus Christ and Him crucified. The preaching should always point people toward the altar with expectancy in their hearts to receive what they need from God! If you preach the Gospel with anointing, you will experience a powerful altar service. If you teach on giving, the altar service will more than likely be short and sweet, but prayerfully, the plate will be a bit heavier next week.

To some, preaching the Word is foolishness, but never underestimate the power of preaching the Word of God. Just as the high priest needed the table of shewbread before he entered into the Holy of Holies, we need the Bread of Life to prepare our hearts for an encounter with the Almighty. Good preaching always convicts hearts, challenges thinking, builds faith, and gives hope to those who receive it. God has chosen preaching as His method of revealing His saving power to mankind.

1 Corinthians 1:18-21

> 18 For the preaching of the cross is to them that perish foolishness; but unto us which are saved **it is the power of God.**
>
> 19 For it is written, I will destroy the wisdom of the wise, and will bring to nothing the understanding of the prudent.

> 20 Where is the wise? where is the scribe? where is the disputer of this world? hath not God made foolish the wisdom of this world?
>
> 21 For after that in the wisdom of God the world by wisdom knew not God, **it pleased God by the foolishness of preaching to save them that believe.**

At times, the move and anointing of the Holy Spirit is so strong that it takes over the service. These are rare and wonderful services; however, remember that people need to hear the Word of God so don't allow it as the norm. The Word of God prepares and draws hearts to receive the Gospel. This is the method that God has ordained since biblical times when Peter preached his first sermon at Pentecost. Just as in that day, anointed preaching produces a positive, powerful response that draws people to the altar to receive from God.

Trained, Compassionate Altar Workers

Every church needs to have a trained altar team in place ready to minister. If you do not have an altar team, you need to train one. Every church has Christians who are compassionate to the needs of the people and these folks are usually more sensitive and skilled at talking with people during serious moments in life. The people working the altar need to be full of the Holy Ghost and sensitive to the moving of the Spirit. Some Christians are prayer warriors and possess spiritual gifts of faith, healing and spiritual discernment that are needed to minister at the altar. These are the people who should lead your altar team.

Whenever Jesus laid hands on somebody, He was moved with compassion before He prayed. Compassion touches the heart of God and is an important element in every altar service! When Phillip preached to the people of Samaria, the people believed, repented and were baptized in Jesus Name, but the Holy Ghost had not yet fallen on any of them. So what happened? They sent for Peter and John to lay hands on them and pray for them to receive the Holy Ghost. Peter and John, who happened to be the closest disciples to Jesus, probably had more faith...they were the first altar workers in Pentecost.

The altar team also needs to be sensitive to the type of altar call the speaker has initiated. Some altar calls are for the infilling of the Holy Ghost, and sometimes the speaker may have some specific instructions about repentance, faith, and yielding to the Spirit.

If the altar call is just an open call for all to come, don't hesitate to ask people what their needs are. Some need to repent, some need healing, some need restoration and some just need for a fellow believer to intercede for and with them. Don't assume to know their need. Let them know that you are there to pray. You can only do that if you know what their need is.

There are times, however, when a person approaches the altar for a personal time of repentance or prayer. Remind your altar workers to be sensitive to the needs of others in that way as well. At those times, the altar workers should pray for them while allowing them space to seek God one-on-one.

In the Closing Moments

The end of an altar service is also a good time to baptize people. This can revitalize the altar service and conclude the service on a positive note. This leaves the congregation with a spirit of expectancy and joy, maintaining momentum.

Not every service requires a dismissal prayer. Simply remind folks to greet one another and introduce themselves to guests, and tell them they're dismissed. However, if it is a Bible study night and no altar call is given, a dismissal prayer will reinforce the teaching of that service.

To summarize, here is an outline to review what we have just discussed:

Order of Service:
1. Welcome and announcements. This could also include a brief meet and greet.
2. Opening prayer.
3. Praise and Worship.
4. Tithe and offering.
5. Prayer for immediate needs of assembly.
6. Special singing or a slow worship chorus.
7. Preaching of the Word.
8. Altar Service.

Momentum Stoppers:
- No prayer for the service.
- A lack of timing and order of service.
- Announcements given in the middle of service.
- Verbal prayer requests.
- Open testimony services.
- Leaders who like to preach every time they get a microphone in their hands.

- Too many preliminaries of any sort.
- Unprepared in heart and mind who disrupt or quench God's Spirit.
- No altar workers at the altars.

Guard Your Virtue

On the way to heal Jairus' daughter, Jesus had a crowd surround Him. A woman, who had an issue of blood for 12 years, pressed through the throng to touch His garment.

Mark 5:30

> 30 And Jesus, **immediately knowing in himself that virtue had gone out of him,** turned him about in the press, and said, Who touched my clothes?

The Scriptures tell us that the very moment the woman touched Jesus' garment, virtue left Him.

Virtue can mean any good or positive attribute of a person. But in this case, the Greek word for virtue is "dunamis" which specifically means **miraculous power.**

When the woman touched Jesus, the miracle-working power of God immediately went out of Him. He felt it leave. Yes, the woman was immediately healed, and yes, Jesus had enough virtue left in Him to go and heal Jairus' daughter. Consider, though, if it had been Peter or John. Would they have had enough virtue left to heal Jairus' daughter? Perhaps not.

(Dave's thoughts)

As a pastor, I step to the pulpit all prayed up. I fast, study and I seek God's will for that particular service. People wait for the service to start and visitors, who need the Holy Ghost, are in the house. I see the hunger and the needs and I am ready to minister to those needs. Then out of nowhere, a church member, who hasn't prayed and fasted or sought God, blindsides me. He or she wants my ear for one reason or another. Most times, it is not a spiritual need nor is it important in the scope of eternity. Nine times out of ten, what they want to discuss could wait for another time and place. Yet they feel what they have to say is important enough to distract the man of God at a very important juncture. In essence, they try to steal my virtue.

(Jim's thoughts)

I wish I had a dollar for every time someone informed me about a clogged toilet just as I walk into the sanctuary to preach....seriously! They don't do that intentionally; they just don't know any better. Satan uses them to steal the anointing, to steal the miracle-working power of God for that service.

Every preacher knows exactly what I'm talking about. You were full of virtue, but then it was drained; now you struggle to regain the Spirit. Realizing this, you rush back to your office, fall on your knees in prayer, and try to refocus and refuel. I would recommend that all preachers do the meeting and greeting after a service to reduce the possibility of this happening on a regular basis.

Actually, teaching about virtue and the importance of a focused service is a good topic for one of your ministry teams to teach at a midweek Bible study night!

In Conclusion

Our altars are the place where man meets God in all His fullness. It is our job and responsibility to gear ourselves and our ministries to win our world to Christ and bless believers with God's anointing. That takes prayer, preparation, and action. The anointing breaks the yokes of bondage, and it begins at the altar.

CHAPTER NINE

Momentum in Leadership

As a leader, how many times have you enthusiastically started a new project, excited about its prospects? Eager to begin, you call together your leadership teams, make plans and set the project in motion. But one thing lacks...you've forgotten to answer the questions that need answering.

Starting new ventures is great for creating momentum; however, before you begin, you must ask yourself and your team leaders if the project is sustainable in the long run. In other words, can you finish what you start? What's more, if the right people aren't in place to make it happen, it is more beneficial to refrain from starting until you have the appropriate people trained to take on the new project.

THE LEADERSHIP OF JESUS

In everything, Jesus is our example, and momentum in leadership is no exception. Jesus looked ahead. His death, burial, resurrection and ascension into heaven were just a few short years away. In order for the church to succeed without Him, He trained and positioned the right people in the right place, ready to carry on His ministry after His ascension.

Often Jesus said, "My hour is not yet come," or "It is not yet my time." He walked in sync with God's will and timing, cognizant of the preparation needed to complete His earthly tasks. And He made sure His disciples were equipped to continue His ministry after He left this Earth.

The Lord is the finest example of leadership we will ever hope to have. His calling and training of the twelve disciples is a model of perfect leadership in ministry. Through Jesus' leadership style, we can gain a sense of what it takes to create momentum in our ministries. The momentum Jesus created with His twelve disciples still moves forward today, 2000 years later.

By the time Jesus began His ministry and summoned the twelve disciples in Matthew 10, He was halfway into His ministry. That meant that Jesus had approximately two years to train twelve men to carry on the work that He had started just months prior to their calling.

Jesus' ministry had two phases. In the first portion of His ministry, He labored single-handedly for over a year. His miracles and teachings were, for the most part, limited to the area of Galilee. As Jesus gained followers, it became clear that He would travel greater distances to reach and teach greater numbers of people. This large group would be unable to follow Jesus wherever He went, especially over the long journeys that became part of His later ministry.

Jesus needed a certain few with Him at all times. He needed to reproduce Himself in a group of willing and faithful men who would be able to carry on His ministry to the world. Thus, Jesus called the twelve disciples.

Mark 3:13-19

> 13 And he goeth up into a mountain, **and calleth unto him whom he would: and they came unto him.**
>
> **14 And he ordained twelve, that they should be with him, and that he might send them forth to preach,**
>
> **15 And to have power to heal sicknesses, and to cast out devils:**
>
> 16 And Simon he surnamed Peter;
>
> 17 And James the son of Zebedee, and John the brother of James; and he surnamed them Boanerges, which is, The sons of thunder:
>
> 18 And Andrew, and Philip, and Bartholomew, and Matthew, and Thomas, and James the son of Alpheus, and Thaddeus, and Simon the Canaanite,
>
> 19 And Judas Iscariot, which also betrayed him: and they went into a house.

For the final two years of His life, Jesus focused on these men. The crowds grew to greater numbers than before. Jesus would still perform miracles, but if the momentum was to continue, He had to direct His passion toward these twelve ordinary men. For several years, Jesus trained simple and common people: Fishermen, carpenters, a tax-collector, a zealot and tradesmen. They were all as ordinary as you and I.

How did Jesus select these twelve men? First and foremost, He prayed. In fact, the Bible records that Jesus continued in prayer all night long.

Luke 6:12-13

> 12 And it came to pass in those days, **that he went out into a mountain to pray, and continued all night in prayer to God.**

> 13 And when it was day, he called unto him his disciples: and of them he chose twelve, whom also he named apostles;

Jesus had already developed a pattern of prayer in His life. Many times, He retreated to a mountain to escape the pressures and hustles of life. The Greek language uses only one word for this event—"dianuktereuo"—which means to sit up the entire night. For eight to ten hours, Jesus prayed. Interestingly, most of us struggle to pray for one hour! Do you remember the last time you stayed awake all night in prayer?

For over a year, Jesus was familiar with the men He would call. Jesus prayed for these men's souls, their futures, their safety, their understanding and their faith. He prayed for them to develop spiritually into an unstoppable force that would impact the world. We know from Scripture that what Jesus prayed for came to fruition.

Jesus faced controversy from the very beginning of His ministry. His own community literally tried to kill Him after He taught in the local synagogue. Shortly after this, He became popular among the people in the region of Galilee. As the word spread of His teachings and His miracles, huge crowds of people flocked to see and hear Him. The crowds grew so large that He would occasionally teach from a boat on the Sea of Galilee just to get away from the press of people.

Jesus was no doubt the most popular figure who existed in this region at that time. What's worth noting though, is that Jesus did nothing to use His popularity to advance His cause or gain momentum. In fact, He did the opposite.

Imagine the crowds He could have drawn had He concentrated on marketing His Name? What would have happened had

He conceded to some of the religious leaders' demands? But none of that interested Jesus.

Jesus was controversial for sure. At times, His teachings and messages were so offensive that almost everyone left Him except His faithful few.

John 6:60-67

> 60 Many therefore of his disciples, when they had heard this, said, **This is a hard saying; who can hear it?**
>
> 61 When Jesus knew in himself that his disciples murmured at it, he said unto them, **Doth this offend you?**
>
> 62 What and if ye shall see the Son of man ascend up where he was before?
>
> 63 It is the spirit that quickeneth; the flesh profiteth nothing: the words that I speak unto you, they are spirit, and they are life.
>
> 64 But there are some of you that believe not. For Jesus knew from the beginning who they were that believed not, and who should betray him.
>
> 65 And he said, Therefore said I unto you, that no man can come unto me, except it were given unto him of my Father.
>
> **66 From that time many of his disciples went back, and walked no more with him.**
>
> **67 Then said Jesus unto the twelve, Will ye also go away?**

Only the twelve simple men stayed with Jesus after everyone else left. It was then that Jesus chose these twelve to mentor, train and disciple over the next two years.

John 15:16
> 16 Ye have not chosen me, but I have chosen you, and ordained you, that ye should go and bring forth fruit, and that your fruit should remain: that whatsoever ye shall ask of the Father in my name, he may give it you.

TRAINING THE TWELVE

By now, Jesus' ministry had reached a point of no return. The religious leaders of the day made up their minds to kill Him and make an example of Him. The hunt was on and time was short. Wherever Jesus went, He worked quickly, getting in and out before He was discovered. The crucifixion was only a few years away and He needed to prepare His twelve disciples to carry on His message.

This two-year period of time was critical to maintain and advance the momentum Jesus established in the first year of His ministry. From this point forward, the whole character and motive of Jesus' ministry changed. His focus switched from the multitudes to the few. His first priority was to train the men who would become His ambassadors of the Gospel and the momentum would continue through these chosen few.

Twelve is a significant number because anything less than that would have been insufficient to maintain the revival that started at Pentecost; it would end as quickly as it started. However, the 12 grew into 70, then 120, and eventually into 3,000 people. A little while later, over 5,000 were added to the church.

One hundred and twenty people would have been far too many people to lead and train properly. But twelve was a number Jesus could disciple, mentor, tutor, and teach in a one-on-one setting. Twelve was the number with whom He could have friendship and a relationship.

Less is More

The Lord understood that spending more time with less people would eventually impact the Kingdom in a greater measure than meeting with great crowds of people. Less would become more...many, many more. All of us need to use this concept in training and mentoring other leaders.

Jesus took it a step further. He broke down the twelve into three. Peter, James, and John became what we know as the inner circle; they were the closest to Jesus. These three were instrumental in carrying on what Jesus started. Whatever these three did, the others would also do. Consequently, Jesus spent more time mentoring these three than any of the other nine disciples.

- Peter was the one to whom Jesus entrusted the keys of the Kingdom. He went on to preach the keynote message at Pentecost.
- John was the disciple whom Jesus loved. The Lord shared things with John that he never shared with the others. Many of those things are recorded in the Gospel of John and the Book of Revelation.
- James and John were known as the Sons of Thunder, possessing a zeal for God that the others did not have.

Jesus had deeper discussions with these three men and they were closer to the Master that the others. For example, Jesus asked Peter, James and John to join Him when He healed Jairus' daughter. They were present during the transfiguration and as Jesus anguished in the Garden of Gethsemane. They were the first great leaders of the church and became the foundation with Jesus as the Chief Cornerstone.

Jesus Christ, God of this universe, concentrated the majority of His efforts on three men who would emerge as the leaders of His Church. With Jesus as their commanding officer, these three men experienced hands-on training in the front lines of a spiritual warfare.

As we follow Jesus' example, we too, will realize that less is more. After all, we can train and mentor a few a lot better than we can mentor a whole group or a classroom of potential leaders.

In everything we do, we should keep these concepts in mind. Don't start something that you cannot properly manage and maintain. It will fail, having wasted precious time, energy, and resources to no avail. Simplification is key to maintaining momentum in any given organization.

The Leadership of Joshua

Another example of sound leadership, is Joshua. In just a short amount of time, Joshua accomplished what Moses failed to achieve in 40 years of effort. He was first known as a servant of Moses. The King James Version of the Bible actually described Joshua using the word "minister," which means to serve or to wait on.

Exodus 24:13

> 13 And Moses rose up, **and his minister Joshua:** and Moses went up into the mount of God.

Before a leader can lead, he must serve. Joshua wasn't called a servant of God until he actually conquered Canaan. It took 40 years of service to Moses and Aaron before Joshua moved into a leadership position. He was not only willing to serve, but he lived to serve.

Exodus 33:11

> 11 And the Lord spake unto Moses face to face, as a man speaketh unto his friend. And he turned again into the camp: **but his servant Joshua, the son of Nun, a young man, departed not out of the tabernacle.**

Serving Moses was Joshua's passion. His desire to serve was so intense that he refused to depart from the tabernacle. The lesson to us is that we will never become great leaders until we first become great servants.

PASSING OF THE MANTLE

Think about the task facing Joshua at the time of Moses' death.

Deuteronomy 34:9-12

> 9 And Joshua the son of Nun was full of the spirit of wisdom; for Moses had laid his hands upon him: and the children of Israel hearkened unto him, and did as the Lord commanded Moses.

> 10 And **there arose not a prophet since in Israel like unto Moses,** whom the Lord knew face to face,
>
> 11 In all the signs and the wonders, which the Lord sent him to do in the land of Egypt to Pharaoh, and to all his servants, and to all his land,
>
> 12 And in all that mighty hand, and in all the great terror which Moses shewed in the sight of all Israel.

When it came to leadership, Moses was the man. Nobody compared to him. No one could lead like Moses; after all, Moses had spent 40 days with God on Mount Sinai. Still, Moses was a man who had fulfilled his time. Moses—the hero of the people—had passed the mantle to Joshua. After 40 years of wandering, Joshua rallied the people together and convinced them to possess the land.

Imagine how Joshua must have felt and the thoughts that ran through his mind. Israel stood at the brink of obtaining their promised land, the swollen Jordan River was before them, and 40 years had passed since they last stood there and failed. Now God chose and ordained Joshua to do what Moses couldn't do.

It's safe to say that Joshua needed a little encouragement from the Lord....

Joshua 1:1-7

> 1 Now after the death of Moses the servant of the Lord it came to pass, that the Lord spake unto Joshua the son of Nun, Moses' minister, saying,
>
> 2 **Moses my servant is dead; now therefore arise, go over this Jordan, thou, and all this people, unto the land which I do give to them, even to the children of Israel.**

> 3 Every place that the sole of your foot shall tread upon, that have I given unto you, as I said unto Moses.
>
> 4 From the wilderness and this Lebanon even unto the great river, the river Euphrates, all the land of the Hittites, and unto the great sea toward the going down of the sun, shall be your coast.
>
> 5 There shall not any man be able to stand before thee all the days of thy life: as I was with Moses, so I will be with thee: I will not fail thee, nor forsake thee.
>
> 6 Be strong and of a good courage: for unto this people shalt thou divide for an inheritance the land, which I sware unto their fathers to give them.
>
> 7 Only be thou strong and very courageous, that thou mayest observe to do according to all the law, which Moses my servant commanded thee: turn not from it to the right hand or to the left, that thou mayest prosper whithersoever thou goest.

In this writing, Joshua felt alone; he shouldered the weight that Moses had carried for so long. Now he is leader to nearly 3 million people and they await his direction. Joshua has no momentum on which to ride; Israel has wandered in circles for 40 years. Yet Joshua obeys God and follows His instructions.

Joshua's Obedience Sets the Stage

God commanded Joshua to, "Go over this Jordan River and possess this land," and that is what Joshua set out to do. First he sent two spies to the great fortress city of Jericho and they returned with a good report. They could take the land.

The word on the street was that Jericho feared these wandering people. Jericho's inhabitants heard about the mighty works Israel's God had done for and through them. They heard about the miracles of deliverance and now these people stood at their doorstep. Needless to say, Jericho was alarmed.

Joshua 2:20
> 24 And they said unto Joshua, **Truly the Lord hath delivered into our hands all the land;** for even all the inhabitants of the country do faint because of us.

Contrast this report with the twelve spies who went into the land 40 years earlier. Ten returned with an evil report and God cursed them and caused them to wander in the wilderness one year for every day they were in the land. Imagine what would have happened if these two spies had brought back an evil report? We will never know, but God may well have sent them back into the wilderness. This was one small victory to build upon and it started the ball rolling in the right direction. It built confidence and hope and the momentum began.

When Joshua received the good news, he dispatched the priests, carrying the Ark of God to the Jordan River. There he instructed all of Israel to watch the Ark.

When the Ark of God and the priests entered the river, it would signal all of Israel to cross over. The moment the priests' feet touched the water, the river pushed back and the entire nation of Israel passed through on dry ground.

Joshua's obedience set the stage for a miracle of God to prepare the way for Israel to enter into the Promised Land. Joshua was prepared to move forward despite the cost, but the Lord was with him. God dried up the waters of the flooded Jordan and they crossed on dry ground. Now, Israel had back-to-back victories on which to build. They all stood on the land God promised them and their faith soared, ready to do whatever Joshua asked.

What Joshua did next is worth noting. He asked one man from each of the twelve tribes to take a stone from the Jordan where the priests had stood, and bring it to the camp. Then Joshua assembled the stones to build a memorial to the Lord for His faithfulness in leading them into the Promised Land.

Joshua 4:21-24

> 21 And he spake unto the children of Israel, saying, When your children shall ask their fathers in time to come, saying, What mean these stones?
> 22 Then ye shall let your children know, saying, Israel came over this Jordan on dry land.
> 23 For the Lord your God dried up the waters of Jordan from before you, until ye were passed over, as the Lord your God did to the Red sea, which he dried up from before us, until we were gone over:
> 24 That all the people of the Earth might know the hand of the Lord, that it is mighty: that ye might fear the Lord your God for ever.

The stones served as a reminder to their children and their grandchildren of how God delivered them through the Jordan River and the Red sea on dry ground. The stones were an eternal memorial before God.

Remembering and sharing with your children and others what God has achieved in your life is a living memorial to His faithfulness. We can maintain momentum in our churches by celebrating past victories and awesome answers to prayer.

The Bible goes on to say...

Joshua 4:13

> 14 On that day the Lord magnified Joshua in the sight of all Israel; and they feared him, as they feared Moses, all the days of his life.

Part of gaining momentum as a leader is to gain the confidence of the people. The people need to see your courage, faith and passion. They need to see you are willing to press forward regardless of the circumstances or the consequences! If you exhibit that kind of confidence and faith, folks will follow you without hesitation.

An element to this story that is not often discussed, is that Joshua disallowed the Israelites to celebrate upon entering the Promise Land. In a society that commemorates everything, many of us would have announced a holiday! But not Joshua. He still had things to do. He ordered circumcision according to God's law for the children of Israel. At the Jordan River, they rested until they were whole. After that, the people kept the Passover on the fourteenth day of the month in the plains of Jericho. In every area, Joshua followed every jot and tittle of God's commands. As a result, momentum grew in everything they did as they gained favor with God through Joshua's leadership.

ISRAELITES' PROMISED LAND

Joshua 5:9

> 9 And the Lord said unto Joshua, This day have I rolled away the reproach of Egypt from off you. Wherefore the name of the place is called Gilgal unto this day.

The faith of the people soared and the past was behind them. A time of prosperity had come for Israel. From that day forward they no longer ate manna; they ate the fruit of the land of Canaan, their Promised Land. Victory was at hand, they were ready to do battle and the city of Jericho was in their sights!

Jericho was one of the greatest fortress cities in the land of Canaan. The Bible says that the men were mighty men of valor, yet because of the miracles that accompanied the children of Israel, Jericho hid behind the walls.

The battle of Jericho is one of the most remembered Sunday school stories of all time. Yet it really wasn't a battle at all; rather, a display of the omnipotence of God demonstrated through His chosen people. The men of war were directed to march around Jericho one time each day for six days. On the seventh day they marched around the city seven times. On the seventh time, the priests were instructed to blow their trumpets and it was at that moment that God brought down the city. This victory was clearly a confirmation that God was with Joshua and his people. It was the beginning of many great victories to come.

Yes, God was responsible for the victory, but they would have never achieved it had Joshua not established obedience to God as his first priority. From the day Moses died until this day, Israel has experienced success after success and Jericho's defeat was by far their greatest victory.

From that moment on, Israel never looked back. Under the leadership of Joshua, Israel marched through Canaan victorious. City after city fell to the army of Israel. King after king was defeated. Momentum was on her side and she was an unstoppable force. All in all, the armies of Joshua and Israel defeated 31 kings and each victory was easier than the one before because of the momentum gained through Joshua's obedience to God.

In Conclusion

As much as God brought victory and success through numerous miracles, the real momentum started inside the heart and mind of Joshua. That's where momentum begins today, too—in the hearts and minds of leaders who possess a passion to do great things for God.

The momentum began with Joshua's vision to reinforce the people as a result of his obedience to and passion for God, and to do so with courage and all of his might. However, it was his obedience that activated the flow of momentum.

Since momentum is part of God's nature, as we obey Him, He always comes through for us and things naturally begin to happen according to His will. That is what happened at Jericho and will happen in our lives and ministries the moment we follow the will of God and press forward as true leaders of the Lord.

CHAPTER TEN

Momentum Balance

There is a definite balance between man-made momentum and God-ordained momentum. In this chapter, we'll explore the relationship between the two.

JOSHUA'S EXAMPLE

In Chapter 9 we discussed how Joshua—through his obedience to God—was able to gain a lot of momentum in a brief period of time. Obeying God was his first and foremost priority and he had God in mind with every decision he made. Joshua knew that God valued obedience over sacrifice and he lived his life accordingly. A God-ordained momentum moved in Joshua's life because of his obedience to the Lord.

That is not to say that Joshua did not establish any momentum on his own. It was clear that early in Joshua's life, the crowd's opinion failed to influence him. Of the twelve spies that were sent out, Joshua was one of only two that brought back a good report. He was a leader from the very beginning; he had vision and passion and he acted decisively. He was unafraid to stand up for what he believed and he demonstrated courage and conviction.

Without a doubt, if Joshua had not been a man of God, he still would have been a leader—people would have followed him to the death. Yet Joshua trusted God more than anything else in his life, including his leadership qualities. He was careful not to let his own passion and pride interfere with God's plan for Israel.

Often, our ministry's momentum is derailed simply because we disobeyed God, while other times we depend on our own vision, passion, talents or ideas. However, what would or could happen if we tapped into God's ordained momentum? To achieve the greatest amount of success we must submit all of our dreams, visions, and goals to God's ultimate plan for His people.

Two Kings, Different Momentums

God chose and anointed the first two kings of Israel. Each one of them began their reigns empowered by God, and through their obedience, each one tapped into God's momentum.

The prophet Samuel anointed the first king, Saul. At first, Saul obeyed God. He became king at a time of confusion in Israel. There was no kingdom, so Saul—with God's anointing—created one; there was no army, so he created that, too.

Saul won battle after battle, victory after victory. The power of God was on his side, yet lurking within Saul's heart was a passion not of God. He enjoyed his power too much and became proud and jealous of his position. As time passed, Saul became obsessed with his own plans and desires for Israel.

Over time, the momentum with which God blessed Saul dissipated, until it totally vanished. Saul's jealousy and thirst for power turned him into a raving madman, obsessed with finding and killing the one who God had chosen to replace him. Saul, the once anointed of the Lord, even stooped so low as to consult with witches. So God spoke through the witch and His message was simple: Saul's reign was finished. Immediately, God's momentum halted in Saul's life.

The second king, David, was also anointed by Samuel the prophet. David's entrance to the throne began a little differently than Saul's. David's leadership training began in the meadows and hilltops of his father's fields and it continued in the caves and forests while he ran for his life.

During that time, Saul did everything within his power to take David's life; however, David never raised a hand against Saul. Even when the opportunity presented itself to him, David said, "I will not raise my hand against the anointed of the Lord." David somehow understood that if he took Saul's life, he would become just like him. He understood that only God had the power to appoint and remove kings. If God wanted to remove Saul, then God would be the One to do so, not David. David had experienced incredible momentum in his life and ministry, and wisely, he was not about to do something that would hinder that momentum. David's dreams and passion were surrendered to God totally.

What transpired next is a lesson for all of us. The men, who once were loyal to Saul, slowly began to leave him. One by one, they saw that Saul had lost his mind and that God's anointing had left the king's life. A few men turned into dozens, and then hundreds turned to David and followed him.

David did not recruit them; he had nothing to offer them. All he could offer them was the same fugitive lifestyle he was living. At first they sought David because they hated Saul. Eventually they saw in David what they needed to see in Saul; namely, a deep and passionate love for God. The men recognized that God's blessing and anointing was no longer on Saul's life, but on David's.

These men were a sorry bunch of fellows. They consisted of criminals, thieves, liars and fugitives. David did not try to lead them, for you can't lead men like this. Instead, David kept his eyes on God; he sang of his love for God and prayed often. Through personal example, David taught what loving and having a passion for God was. Before long, the men's hearts and lives began to change and they followed David, not out of obligation, but out of love. They developed a love for God and a love and respect for this man who obeyed God alone.

This band of misfits was known as "David's Mighty Men," 600 strong. These men were the most loyal men in the kingdom of Israel and together they changed the course of world history.

Now, the change in momentum that swung in David's favor didn't happen overnight, but over a period of a few years. Finally, at Saul's death, David was crowned king of Israel. God would fulfill his plan through David, the one who was so dear to God's heart.

Fast forward almost 40 years. One of David's sons, Absalom, listened to the wrong people. They filled his mind with seeds of rebellion and pride saying, "Absalom, you have the answers. Your father is too old; he can't relate anymore. It's your time now." As a result, the kingdom suffered many problems and eventually Absalom conceded and agreed to take the kingdom from his father.

David, though, does something amazing—something most of us would never do. Undoubtedly, we would try to stop this rebellion, right? Not in David's mind.

David could have done what Saul had done to him and hunted down Absalom. Instead, David relented and said, "This is not my kingdom, it is God's." He reasoned that perhaps his time was up; maybe his sin was too great. I am sure that David wanted to remain king, but he set his desires aside and said, "God, this is for you to decide." David was not about to get in the way of God's momentum.

So David took all of his family and his 600 mighty men and left town. They refused to fuss or fight. Then David sent Zadok the priest and his two sons back to Jerusalem with the ark of God. His instructions were simple, "Carry the ark back into the city: If God wants me back in Jerusalem, please let me know; if He doesn't, then let God do with me as He wishes."

2 Samuel 15:25-28

> 25 And the king said unto Zadok, **Carry back the ark of God into the city: if I shall find favour in the eyes of the Lord, he will bring me again, and shew me both it, and his habitation:**
>
> **26 But if he thus say, I have no delight in thee; behold, here am I, let him do to me as seemeth good unto him.**
>
> 27 The king said also unto Zadok the priest, Art not thou a seer? return into the city in peace, and your two sons with you, Ahimaaz thy son, and Jonathan the son of Abiathar.
>
> 28 See, **I will tarry in the plain of the wilderness, until there come word from you to certify me.**

David placed everything in the Lord's hands. *"Lord, not my will, but Thine be done."* He chose to have no part in this fight unless God approved of it, even though he knew Absalom was unfit to be king. After all, David had already arranged for Solomon to reign in his stead. Yet, he set aside his desires and allowed God to make the decisions, giving the Lord room in which to work.

When we truly submit our plans to God, He will make them all work out in the long run. David refused to allow his own desires or agenda to interrupt the momentum that God had created in his life, and so must we. Then perhaps we, too, might be called "a man after God's own heart."

CHAPTER ELEVEN

Momentum in Preaching

Jesus was on His way to heal a young child when a woman with an issue of blood reached out in faith to touch Him. Instantly, she was healed. Feeling the virtue (anointing) leave Him, Jesus asked, "Who touched me?"

Luke 8:45-46

> 45 And Jesus said, Who touched me? When all denied, Peter and they that were with him said, Master, the multitude throng thee and press thee, and sayest thou, **Who touched me?**
> 46 And Jesus said, **Somebody hath touched me: for I perceive that virtue is gone out of me.**

SUSTAINING GOD'S VIRTUE AND ANOINTING

As ministers, we know that people extract our spiritual strength and virtue much like the woman who touched Jesus in the above passage. It comes with the territory. People will phone you at any time of the day or night, or unexpectedly show up at your home. They will tell you their problems at the grocery store and think nothing of holding you captive with conversation before church begins. By the time you step to the pulpit, you often feel spiritually spent. Preaching itself drains us of our virtue when we preach under God's anointing.

Both of us (Jim and Dave) have worked many hard and long hours in the construction field most of our lives. Yet, rarely do we feel as tired and exhausted as we do after we preach an anointed sermon. Jesus Himself experienced times when He retreated from the crowd and even from His close followers to get alone with the Father. This is where Jesus' virtue (anointing) was restored.

Nothing replaces personal prayer and time alone with the Source of virtue. Prayer, fasting and constant communion are an absolute necessity if you desire to maintain the anointing of God. A preacher without virtue is like a mechanic without tools. He can tell you what's wrong, but he can't help you very much. We need God's virtue and anointing to minister to those attacked by Satan and to heal their physical and spiritual wounds.

Let's face it, preaching without virtue is just oratory. The sermon might grab interest but if it fails to produce results in the lives of the hearers, it is of little use. While a well thought-out and prepared message is a necessity, the sermon alone cannot break the yoke. It takes virtue to deliver souls from sin and it takes anointing to break the yoke of bondage in people's lives. Without a saturation of the Spirit on a message, it is little more than a lecture. There is no substitute for the power of God in a preacher's life and ministry. It takes virtue and anointing; it takes prayer.

If all Peter offered the lame man at the gate Beautiful was a good sermon, healing would not have occurred that day. But

Peter had the anointing of God and possessed the goods to get the job done.

What happens when you preach? Do people receive the Holy Spirit? Do they receive deliverance and healing? Does your preaching possess virtue? Or is it just good oratory?

(Jim's thoughts)

Recently a mentor of mine spoke about evangelists who seemed to have a hard time conveying their message. He said he stopped second guessing these evangelists when he observed the results—congregants who flocked to the altar as the Spirit moved. He noted, "Many were saved even though the message was not all that compelling."

Preaching under the anointing of the Holy Spirit is what produces results. As you study and prepare your message, pray and seek God for His anointing. All of the Bible study reference books in the world and a thousand hours of intense study cannot replace your individual time of prayer before the Lord.

Preach It!

People don't use this phrase too much anymore, but years ago folks would cheer on the preacher shouting, "Preach it!" One of the reasons people no longer interact this way is that they seldom hear the kind of preaching that makes them want to encourage the pastor or evangelist for more. Funny stories, jokes, Power Points, and background music are all effective tools to include in our message. Yet admittedly, those elements seldom stir people's hearts to jump to their feet and shout, "Preach it!"

or "Tell me like it is preacher!"; "Tell us what God wants us to hear!"

Something other than a well-planned sermon is needed. When a messenger of God steps behind the sacred desk, he needs confidence that heaven is behind his words and that angels are attentive to his preaching. There ought to be a Holy Ghost boldness that comes over us as we proclaim, "Thus saith the Lord!"

Pastor Mark Cottrill in Bourbon, Indiana, tells the story of the time when an angel came to hear him preach. (Although he doesn't say it that way, that's what occurred.) Here's what happened.

> The church he pastors went through a bit of a down time and he was discouraged. It seemed as if the congregation was just going through the motions and not behind the preaching of the Word like he wished they would be. You may be able to relate.
>
> As the congregation was filing into the auditorium, Pastor Cottrill's wife Jane noticed a tall, handsome, well dressed young Hispanic man come in and sit down in front of Bro. Tom. The visitor had on a three piece, blue pinstriped suit on. Tom had a particular place that he and his wife would sit. There was an open seat right in front of Tom and the young Hispanic man took it. Tom was good at greeting visitors and making them feel welcome.
>
> The service started as it usually did with the musicians and singers leading the congregation in worship.
>
> Then something happened. The young visitor who was sitting in front of Tom jumped to his feet and starting worshiping with all of his heart. Singing loudly, clapping his hands and raising his hands in worship. Jane herself loves to

worship the Lord, but found herself noticing the exuberant worship of the visitor. Jane noticed this man knew all the words of the worship songs and didn't need a song book.

As the service progressed, the visitor continued to worship with each part of the service. However, during the preaching, he became so excited he could not contain himself. While Pastor Cottrill preached what he thought would be "another Sunday night sermon," the guest repeatedly jumped to his feet and shouted out to encourage the preacher. "Yes", "Amen", "Preach It!" He was cheering on the preacher like some people do their favorite team in the Super Bowl.

Jane was so impressed with this visitor's enthusiasm for the Word; she just had to meet him. After the service, she walked over to where the young man had sat but could not find him. She asked Tom if he knew where the guest was as she wanted to find out who he was. (She hoped he would come back.) "No… What young man are you talking about?" Tom Asked. "You know! The visitor that sat right in front of you during the service. You had to see him Tom. He was standing, shouting and praising the Lord through the whole service." "No," Tom said. "There was no one in front of me."

Bewildered, Jane asked everyone who was sitting all around Tom and the visitor. She talked to the ushers and they all said the same thing. "No, they had not seen anyone come in, sit in front of Tom, or worship the way Jane saw him worship." In fact not a single soul in that entire church except the Pastor's wife saw this tall, handsome, well dressed Hispanic young man come into the service and worship God with all his heart and "get behind" the preacher to encourage him with the message.

Who was this person? It really is no mystery. The young man Jane saw that night was an angel of God who visited their church for the express purpose of ushering in the presence of God with worship and encouragement as the pastor preached God's Word.

Only a couple years later, Pastor Cottrill's wife Jane was watching her husband preach in a service and their 3 year old grandson, Dylan, who was sitting on her lap, asked "who is that big man standing behind pawpaw." She asked "what man" because she didn't see anyone else near her husband. Dylan replied once again "that big tall man following pawpaw around on the platform." No doubt angels are all around us worshipping and encouraging us, especially when the Word of God is being brought forth.

Many people fail to understand the enormous pressure and time constraints the average pastor faces. But God does. Just because you had a bad week, a bad day, or a bad five minutes before the church service, doesn't mean that heaven is not attentive to your message. Regardless of how the congregation responds, God's Word is going forth. His Word is sharper than any two-edged sword, able to divide between soul and spirit. We can't do that, but His Word can. Your jokes, funny stories and oratory may not capture or keep the congregation's attention the way you wish it would, but His anointed Word will.

Don't slam the brakes on the momentum of your church by stepping to the pulpit without virtue. Before you walk up those stairs, stand before the throne. Before you proclaim it to the people, petition it before Him. Realize that angels unaware are listening to your message. If angels hear it, chances are, so do demons. And if they are, then a weak sermon void of God's power may do more harm than good. On the other hand, an anointed, powerful, positive Word from God will turn Hell on its heels and the congregation toward the altar.

(Jim's thoughts)

When a church's leadership loses their virtue and zeal, the congregation will soon follow. After a service some time ago, I sat at the back of the church enjoying a few minutes alone when my daughter, Kristi, confronted me and said, "Dad, you don't look very approachable. You have a scowl on your face and you're not greeting or looking at anybody."

I had no idea I presented that kind of persona. I thought I was just having a moment to myself. Yet Kristi's observations reminded me that if the ministry displays a distant attitude or spirit, the congregation will do the same. Moreover, if the congregation does this then every guest that walks through our church doors will feel unwelcomed and not return. Realizing my error, I stood up and started greeting people with a smile and a hand shake.

Anointing is Attractive

During the time that Jesus ministered in this world, people thronged around him. Yes, some came only to be healed but most of them came to see the man. Who was this man that healed the lepers, opened blind eyes and raised the dead? They had never seen a man like this before. In that day, there were physicians who healed and magicians who conjured up spirits, but this man Jesus was different. He was anointed of God; He had virtue; He spoke with authority and boldness.

He dared to stand in the Temple and preach what the Spirit told him. Risking his life, He stood in the city streets and denounced the Pharisees' teachings that had blinded the Jews.

Jesus was strong and stood tall above the crowd, not due to his stature, but because of his persona. Jesus caught people's attention and He spoke directly to them. The opinions of the majority didn't faze Him; instead, He allowed the Spirit of God to operate through Him in every situation, regardless of the person or circumstances. Whether He addressed the prostitute in the street or the divorcee at the well, Jesus met each individual at the point of their need, speaking the words they needed to hear.

Jesus' preaching oozed with momentum. His words declared and announced the words of the Father and He never apologized for His zeal or authoritative tone. When he spoke, He did so with the knowledge that heaven backed up His every word.

Throughout the New Testament, other men displayed incredible authority with virtue that attracted the crowds. Men like Peter and Paul had no concern for their lives and preached the Name of Jesus to a world that stood ready to persecute them for their beliefs.

In the Word of God and in many churches today, people are often healed and filled with the Holy Spirit while the preacher preaches. More often, they walk and sometimes run to the altar before the sermon is finished or an altar call is given. Their faith or conviction is so strong that they cannot wait until the close of the message to receive what God has for them. That's the kind of preaching our generation, our world, needs to hear.

When people search for a church to attend and for the man who will pastor them, they look for someone who is decisive and confident in his calling. They look for someone who has the answers to their life's problems. They look for a person who is close to God and has virtue and authority in their walk with Him.

People with genuine needs will not stay where their needs are unmet. Many folks are desperate, realizing they need God's help. If they don't find help where they are, they'll go somewhere else to find it. If you have desperate people in your congregation, you have a church on the verge of revival. Desperate people are appreciative of help; they are fantastic worshippers, and they tell others about the good things that are finally happening in their lives. They get excited about living for God and that excitement becomes contagious to the other congregants. This in turn generates visitors, which in turn causes a continuum of the entire process. Growth and revival are the end results.

That's how momentum works. It doesn't stop. It keeps moving. And who would have thought that it all started with a preacher?

CHAPTER TWELVE

Creating Momentum: Team Effort and Old Paths

Winning takes team effort. Creating the kind of momentum that produces a win in sports is much like the kind we need in ministry. In the natural world momentum is, in large part, a study of physics that we associate with the physical. Since nothing is more physical than sports, the concept of momentum applies well as we use physical comparisons to illustrate spiritual momentum.

(Dave's thoughts)

When I think about creating momentum in sports, my mind travels back to my favorite sport—ice hockey. I was brought up in the "Great White North" playing hockey and one of the things I love about it most is that this sport allows its teams to create momentum for themselves in the closing minutes of a game, when they need it the most.

When a team is down by one or two goals—with just a couple of minutes left in the game—they fight to regain momentum, giving their all to try to score and make a last minute comeback. Yet they need something extra—something that will swing the momentum back to them. At this point, something often occurs that doesn't happen in any other sport. The coach, who tries to inspire his team to come from behind, gives the signal to his goalie to come to the bench. This is called "pulling your goalie." Then another player jumps over the boards to join the attack, in essence giving the team an extra skater. With six skaters against five, they work the pressure on the opposing team and hopefully tie the game in the final minutes or seconds.

When they do, they accomplish the impossible; they disrupt the opposing team's momentum and tie up the score in the final minutes of regulation. With the game tied up and the clock winding down, the team has a chance to win the game in overtime. More often than not, that's exactly what happens. Meanwhile, the opposing team plays defensively, scrambling to hold on.

In this scenario the coach has improved his "product" by adding something extra (another skater) from the team that had no momentum. This improvement created enough momentum to make that team successful.

Keep in mind, the coach brought nothing brand new to the game. That extra skater had actually been there all along; yet, the coach found a way to improve on their efforts.

Similarly, we must find ways to improve on what we already have to gain the momentum needed to become successful. Making improvements in ministry is never easy. Yet, if we apply some of the successful concepts used in sports or in the corporate world to our ministries, we will reap some of the same results. In fact, many of these principles are not really new, but are actually biblical principles that have been around for a centuries.

Consider the Team Effort of the Five-Fold Ministry

Ephesians 4:11-13

> 11 And he gave some, apostles; and some, prophets; and some, evangelists; and some, pastors and teachers;
>
> 12 For the **perfecting of the saints, for the work of the ministry, for the edifying of the body of Christ:**
>
> 13 Till we all come in the unity of the faith, and of the knowledge of the Son of God, unto a perfect man, unto the measure of the stature of the fulness of Christ:

From the very first century, God intended for His church to be structured under this plan.

1. Apostles
2. Prophets
3. Evangelists
4. Pastors
5. Teachers

It seems as if our churches lack three or four of these positions. Most young ministers dream of becoming a pastor and some believe that their ministry will reach world status or renowned-evangelist acclaim. Yet the majority of these young men do not feel called to be apostles, teachers, or prophets.

Why is that? Has the fundamental teaching of the basic leadership roles of God's church been diluted? Have we replaced it with our own hierarchical structure, void of balance and the kind of ministry God desires for His Church?

(Jim's thoughts)

Some years ago, soon after I had resigned the pastorate in Chesterton, Indiana, I phoned a few friends in the ministry whom I had known for several years. Natalie and I wanted to take a year off from full-time ministry to regroup, so to speak. At the same time, I didn't want to sit idle if the Lord wanted to use me to minister in other churches. So I phoned some ministers to let them know that I was available to fill in should they need a break or wanted to go on vacation. As a pastor, I knew how much I welcomed and appreciated the opportunity for a seasoned minister to avail himself to give me a break occasionally.

All of my calls were well received. Except one. One young minister quibbled, "Why would I want someone else to evangelize in 'my' church Brother Smith?" "Well," I said, "for one thing it gives the five-fold ministry an opportunity to operate in your church." He responded saying, "Well, I'm the apostle, prophet, evangelist, pastor and teacher in 'my' church." To that I simply wished him well and closed the conversation. Coincidently, this was the same pastor I had invited to speak at our church more than once when he was just starting his speaking ministry.

This pastor thought he could do it all. He was the Superman of "his" church. Unfortunately, as a pastor I have seen this before and so have you. We know that one person cannot do it all. If they try, they will suffer from burn-out and often their family suffers, unable to take the pressure that "doing it all" requires. The spouse will go along with it for awhile and even bask in the romantic notion that his/her spouse runs the church. However, at some point, the pressure will take its toll. And whether the preacher is ready or not, when the spouse is done he/she is done.

A pastor cannot effectively minister in any substantial capacity without the full support of the spouse. You can fake it for awhile, but it won't take the congregation long to realize that the preacher's own spouse and family does not support him/her. Once this is evident, the preacher is finished there.

Experience teaches, however, that we need help if we are ever going to accomplish all that God has called us to do. Admittedly, I am not the smartest guy in the world. I fully realize that I need to surround myself with those who can advise, encourage, instruct and give true spiritual inspiration to not only me but to those who are a part of the organization I lead.

As far as momentum in the church, no team is as good as their best player; they are only as good as their unified effort. Michael Jordan was not the only player on the Bulls when they won six NBA titles. Michael was an incredible player, but without the other ten or eleven players on the team he would have never won a single game. He might have made a few incredible shots, but the overall effort would have failed if he played alone.

"Don't get intoxicated with your own preaching!" Rev. S.G. Norris, who was the president of Apostolic Bible Institute where I attended many years ago, would say this to our class. He meant this—don't allow pride to lure you into thinking that since you preached a good sermon or two, you are the only preacher God uses.

The Importance of the Five-Fold Ministry

If it weren't for the encouragers in your church who reassure disheartened fellow members, eventually you might not have a congregation to preach to.

A great message preached on Sunday night is not enough to produce a well-grounded, stabilized church. Every church needs the five-fold ministry in operation. The message starts the momentum, but others have to keep that momentum going for it to continue.

Sadly, the team effort of the five-fold ministry is missing in most, if not all, churches. But as believers unite and work together there is power, authority, anointing and accountability.

God never intended for pastors to do it all by themselves... it just can't be done. So we need to reject the mindset that we can. Truth is, we all need that extra "skater" to accomplish God's work.

- We need evangelists who can gather and reap the harvest.
- We need prophets who can bring a fresh word from God that breathes new life into the body of Christ.
- We need teachers who can teach truth and lead us into perfection.
- We need apostles who we can submit to and who can lead us in ministry.
- We need pastors who can protect and feed the body of Christ.

As stated before, these are not really new concepts, they just might be new to you or your ministry. God has always planned for His church to operate in this manner but unfortunately, we have strayed from that plan.

The concepts of the five-fold ministry are the same concepts that we shared with you in the world of sports. In baseball, a manager brings in a pinch hitter at the appropriate time of the game just as a coach pulls a goalie to discharge an extra skater, or a coach substitutes a defensive player for an offensive one. These actions are taken to create or maintain momentum on their individual teams. They are performed to attain results.

Certain players have skills that others don't have, and their skills are needed at certain times and places. It is a team effort. That is what the five-fold ministry is all about! Your church can create new momentum by going back to the formula of the first century church; namely, the five-fold ministry. This is not man-made momentum, it is God ordained. It is guaranteed to work because it is part of God's plan and nature.

The Old Ways

In Chapter 4, we shared the story of the Coca-Cola Company. Even though they had success in their original "Classic" formula, they tried to improve on it. Fortunately for them, when their improvement failed to succeed, they had the wherewithal to go back to the original formula and return to what brought them success in the first place. When they did, company sales went through the roof.

In some areas, the church has done the same thing. In our effort to win our world, we strayed from some of the elements that initiated success (momentum) in the early church of the first century. We departed from the old ways primarily in the area of the five-fold ministry. The five-fold ministry is the "Classic" plan of God for all of time. This should never change, and if God's "Classic" plan is not operating in your church, you need to shelve the "new" and bring in the old classic five-fold ministry.

(Dave's Thoughts)

Many of you remember growing up in the church. It was common to attend church four, five and six times a week. That's how our parents were raised. Even in my generation we had revival services five nights a week and twice on Sunday. The travelling evangelist was a huge part of our church and during revival many people came to Christ.

At least once every few months, our District Superintendant stopped by. He was our apostle and prophet, and as he preached we knew his words were straight from the Lord. He brought direction and life into our church and he was also the man who led my father in ministry.

My father was the quintessential pastor and teacher. He taught us, cared for us, and trained us in the nurture and admonition of the Lord. He taught Bible studies to the new converts and gave relevant lessons to the rest of the church. As a result, the Lord added daily to the church such as should be saved.

In this generation of emerging church culture, we must be definitive that what we perceive to be an improvement is still of God. Some of the old ways and old paths that built the church from the onset are still needed today. While society has changed and even our church culture, there is no replacement for some of the basic tenants of living for God or serving in His kingdom.

Ecclesiastes 1:9

> 9 The thing that hath been, it is that which shall be; and that which is done is that which shall be done: **and there is no new thing under the sun.**

G O I N G   B A C K   I S   H A R D

(Dave's thoughts)

The city in which I pastor is filled with people who were, but no longer are, living for God. During the time of my pastorate, many have attended our church and prayed through, but did not stay. It's hard to make your way back. There are so many distractions, too many things competing for your soul. The old ways don't seem the same anymore.

Similarly, it's difficult to create momentum once it's lost. The road back is difficult and long, or as the Bible explains, "the way of the transgressor is hard." The prophet Jeremiah brought the word of the Lord to a people who had strayed from the good old paths of truth...

Jeremiah 6:16

> 16 Thus saith the Lord, **Stand** ye in the ways, and **see**, and **ask** for the old paths, where is the good way, and **walk** therein, and ye shall **find** rest for your souls. But they said, We will not walk therein.

To a country that was once blessed and prosperous, Jeremiah warned the people of their erroneous ways. He instructed them to find the old ways of previous generations that had led their ancestors to prosperity and great blessings. He assured them that not only would they find success, but they would find rest for their souls. What was their response? "We will not walk therein."

The prophet addressed the inherent danger of leaving the "old paths" behind. The danger is this: If you leave behind what brought you success in the first place, you may never get it back.

In this story, Jeremiah used the illustration of a man standing at a road's intersection trying to decide which way to go. This man, who is probably a pilgrim, sees various options before him. There are new roads recently built that are wide and inviting, and some are smaller roads that look narrow and dusty.

But the pilgrim is instructed to find the old road of generations past. When he asks a few travelers the whereabouts of this road, no one seems to have directions; they have no clue of what he is talking about. These people were too concerned about and familiar with the new way. Finally, he finds an older man who looks like he might know. When he asks, the man points him to a very narrow and dirty old path hidden just out of sight. The man states, "That is the good way, don't pay any attention to the road everybody else is taking, walk down this path and you will find rest for your soul."

Jeremiah's Call to Stand, See, Ask, Walk and Find

Finding the old path that you may have left is not an easy process. However, here are four steps that will help you navigate back on course:

1. "Stand" refers to putting yourself in a position where you can consider all of the things before you.
2. "See" refers to keen observation and carefully evaluating all of your options before setting out.
3. "Ask" refers to finding somebody who has experienced the old path who might be able to give you sound advice.

4. "Walk" refers to actually setting out on the old path. As you walk, you will experience some new (new to you) things.

These four steps lead to "find." Finding is the end result, the success of your journey. Here, you will find rest for your soul. You will find success and you will create new momentum in your life and ministry.

Jeremiah directed this prophesy to Judah. Spiritually, Judah was a failure; she was totally backslidden from God. Here is God's description of her...

Jeremiah 5:30-31

> 30 A wonderful and horrible thing is committed in the land;
>
> 31 The prophets prophesy falsely, and the priests bear rule by their means; and my people love to have it so: and what will ye do in the end thereof?

Judah had diverted from the old path. False prophets were everywhere. The priests raped young female worshippers on the steps of the Temple. Shockingly, the people didn't care; in fact, the Bible says that the people loved it. They felt no pressure to live by God's laws and God was not pleased. It was a dark day in Judah and a dark future for them lay ahead.

So Jeremiah's message was not well received. People must have thought he was an old fogey, out of touch and out of sync with the times. Who was this guy asking them to walk in the old paths of their ancestors? Who does he think he is?

You see, Judah was a great and mighty nation at this time. She had been around for hundreds of years and seen great progress in her history. Her people had won many battles, claimed many victories, and the slavery of Egypt was far behind them—almost forgotten. They were the nation that other nations admired and other kings bowed to the King of Judah.

Over the course of time, they had allowed some of the other nations to inter-marry with their children and they embraced some of the pagan cultures and beliefs. Consequently, they had a diversity of religions that worshipped idols and false gods, and they abandoned some of their ancestor's beliefs and traditions. Foolishly, they thought they had it made in the shade; it was an easy life for them.

Then out of nowhere, the prophet Jeremiah preached, "Stand in the way, and see, and ask for the old paths, and walk in the old paths." God's people received him with disdain. In fact, they dismissed him as an insignificant crazy old preacher insisting, "We will not walk in these paths." Little did they know that Babylon would soon attack them, and their sin would drive them back into captivity.

How similar that is today. We live at a time of an emerging church culture, where the new is hip and the old is out. Like the people of Judah, some of us cringe when we hear an old preacher talk about the old ways. Yet those old men and women—our parents and grandparents—experienced some of the greatest revivals of our time because they stuck to the traditional (old ways) of God's Word.

Deuteronomy 32:7

> 7 Remember the days of old, consider the years of many generations: ask thy father, and he will shew thee; thy elders, and they will tell thee.

Let's not be so quick to forsake the old and embrace the new. Rather, stand, see, and ask those great men and women of God who have blazed the trail before us.

Together, let's strive to get back into the game!

CHAPTER THIRTEEN

Creating Momentum: Setting People Up For Success

A GREAT WAY TO CREATE MOMENTUM IN ANY CHURCH IS TO SET PEOPLE UP FOR SUCCESS!

As parents, we train our children to become more confident and when we do, we set them up for success. We desire for them to succeed whether in sports, school, or in just plain problem-solving. When we play games with our kids, we often let them win; other times, we offer clues or hints to the correct answers. When they are babies, we clutch their hands and help them to walk. We do all of these things to help our children gain confidence in their learning skills or in whatever they do in life. This instills in them a momentum that often lasts a lifetime because they learned and developed these skills at an early age.

The bottom line is that we want them to succeed because they are our children. And guess what? God feels the same way about us. He builds our confidence, directs our thoughts, and offers assistance just as we do for our kids. Even when we don't see it, the Lord is acting on our behalf to set us up for success.

In the world, a common business practice is for an employer to give the new employee simple tasks that they know the new person can handle. They want them to succeed because if their employees are successful, so is their company. And success means profits.

In sports, the practice is similar. For instance: A quarterback, transferred from another team or college, must learn an entirely new offense as soon as possible. The offensive coordinator and quarterback coaches do everything they can to get him ready. They show him tapes, teach him, practice the plays and make him memorize the code names of each play.

Yet when it comes to the actual game, they don't just throw him in at the beginning and hope for the best. He may have to watch a veteran quarterback work the system for a few plays. Then when the time is just right, the coach will put in the new quarterback for one short series—just enough to give him a taste of the game and build his confidence in the system. In other words, his coaches want him to succeed, so they position him in the right situation to help that happen.

Some people call this a short-term victory. The long-term victory, of course, is to win the Super Bowl. But if the player can't succeed in the short-term, he will never make the Super Bowl. First he needs a few successful throws. Then when he converts a few "first down" passes, he can put together a successful drive, possibly leading to a touchdown or a field goal. A few of these drives could lead to a victory for the team. Put together a few victories and the team makes the playoffs. Win a few games in the playoffs, and now the team is ready for a Super Bowl Championship!

Ultimate success comes from a series of small wins that lead people to ultimate victory. That is what momentum is...a bunch of small successes that are back-to-back. Every once in a while there may be a setback, but if the successes are greater than the setbacks, you still have momentum. It may be 3 steps forward and 2 steps back, but it is still forward momentum by one step.

KING HEZEKIAH

During the days of King Hezekiah, the people of God backslid from God and His laws. The temple sat in ruins in Jerusalem, the priests were not doing their job, there were no offerings of sacrifice being offered, and only a very few went through the motions of worship.

King Hezekiah came on the scene and when he saw the temple in disrepair, and the people in their apathetic state, he was disgusted. I can imagine him thinking 'where do we start?' They had to start somewhere, why not start with cleaning the temple...

2 Chronicles 29:5

> 5 And said unto them, Hear me, ye Levites, **sanctify now yourselves, and sanctify the house of the Lord God of your fathers, and carry forth the filthiness out of the holy place.**
>
> 16 And the priests went into the inner part of the house of the Lord, to cleanse it, **and brought out all the uncleanness that they found in the temple of the Lord** into the court of the house of the Lord. And the Levites took it, to carry it out abroad into the brook Kidron.
>
> 17 Now they began on the first day of the first month to sanctify, and on the eighth day of the month came they to the porch of the Lord: so they sanctified the house of

the Lord in eight days; and in the sixteenth day of the first month they made an end.

Hezekiah's instructions were simple...clean up the temple, take out the trash, scrub the floors, and repair that which is broken. Although the people were not spiritually ready to offer sacrifices and worship to God, Hezekiah was giving them something that they could handle. They probably didn't realize it, but Hezekiah was setting them up for success. He was building their confidence back up. He was giving them something positive to think about. Hezekiah was giving them a short-term goal that they could see themselves accomplishing without too much trouble. Their success in this short-term effort caused them to re-evaluate their long term goals concerning the Kingdom of God. They now had the desire and the confidence to move on to something greater. Now that the house of God was cleaned up and ready to use, why not go ahead and start using it for what it was intended for? Momentum had been created by the success of a short-term project.

Soon after that, the rulers of the city brought bullocks, rams, lambs, and goats for a sin offering to be made for the atonement of the sins of all the people of Israel. Then they brought the singers and the musicians and they began to sing and worship the Lord. Shortly after that, came the thank offerings and the praise offerings unto the Lord. The Passover was reinstituted, and people that had not served God in generations came back to the Lord with their whole hearts. It all started by a few priests cleaning the mess out of the house of God!

Setting up People for Success in Ministry

We can create momentum in our churches and in our leaders by setting people up for success. In other words don't give them something that they can't handle...build some confidence in them by causing them to be successful! Start small and go from there.

It's important to remember that most, if not all, of those we employ in the area of ministry around the church are volunteers. These are usually not trained ministers. They are not Bible school graduates. For the most part they are carpenters, mechanics, schoolteachers, etc. When you begin working with these people, you soon realize that many of them are going to try to do the work of ministry like they would do their job in their workplace. There is a problem that arises when we began using people in ministry who do not understand true servanthood. We only mention this at this point in our writing, because when we are setting people up for success in ministry, it's important that they realize that success in the church is not the same as success in the workplace.

For example, some people become very successful in the workplace because they have found out how to climb the corporate ladder. There is no corporate ladder in the church. There is only a cross to bear. There is only a servant's towel.

Part of setting somebody up for success is not just showing them how to do a job, but also helping them understand the purpose for which the job is to be done. For example, someone who was a schoolteacher will try to run their Sunday school class like they run their classroom at the junior high. While this can have some good advantages, the teacher could possibly miss the purpose of her ministry as a Sunday school teacher. Without knowing, she may attempt to educate someone rather than teach them spiritual principles.

Another example would be the businessman who sees dollar figures as a rule for success. If this person were allowed to become the treasurer or trustee of the church, he might try to run the church as a corporation instead of a ministry. This person would miss the whole point and purpose of the church, which is to win souls, not to satisfy stockholders.

Setting somebody up for success in ministry involves spending time with them. It means mentoring them and helping them find the place in the church where not only their talents, but also their passion and burden can best be used.

While it is extremely important to use people in areas of the church where they are most qualified, it may not always be in their best interest to place them in an area of ministry simply because they have education or experience for that particular ministry. An example would be somebody who works at a bank or is an accountant. To place them in an area of ministry such as the treasurer of the church, or the person who counts the offering, may not be what is best for that person if their heart is not completely right with God. Someone who works in a bank could easily do some accounting for the church, but it may also cause a problem for them spiritually. They may not be able to handle the knowledge of who is giving and who is not giving.

You may have a carpenter in your church who would be better suited to count the church offerings than a banker...if the carpenter has a closer walk with God than the banker has. Judas is a biblical example of what handling the offerings can do to one's spirit. He may have been good with adding and subtracting, but his walk with God was nowhere near strong enough to handle the responsibility that he was given.

Creating Momentum: Setting People Up For Success

When people fail in the area of ministry, it is very discouraging to them spiritually. There are some deeper reasons for this. Satan loves to focus on our defeats. As any child of God knows, the enemy is always looking for a way to discourage us. He will try to discourage us in our relationship with God. He will try to discourage us in our walk with God and our example before men. And he will try to discourage us in our area of ministry. If he can kill our potential in ministry, then he in essence is killing those whom our ministry could have reached.

Investment in the Kingdom

When you think of the word ministry, think of the word multiplication. Anytime a person comes into ministry, they are in fact being used by God to create multiplication in the church. God will begin to use them to create increase for his kingdom. They become an invested talent.

If you want to kill the true potential of investment, simply cause the principle to decrease. Let's say you have $10.00 that you invest. Let's say your neighbor has $20.00 that he might invest. Both of you can experience a 20% return. Your investment increased by $2.00, but your neighbors investment increased by $4.00. His increase is twice as much as yours. Why? Because he has a greater principle invested.

Every time a person in your church experiences a defeat spiritually, their potential principle is decreased. Each time their own ministry becomes discouraged, their principle for potential is again diminished. Increase the principle and even a small percentage of growth causes the total investment to grow substantially.

A 1% gain is not nearly as good as a 10% gain, but it's better than nothing and it is momentum in the right direction. As well, a 1% gain of an investment principle that is very large is better than a 100% gain of an investment that is very small.

What is the investment principle of the church or ministry you lead? If a number could be put on the number of people, their willingness to serve, desire to support the total vision, etc what would it be? Is there room to increase that number (principle). If we focus on the principle and allow God to worry about the rate of return, our total increase will be much greater.

Too many of us want to see the same rate of growth in our church as the church down the street. The question is, does your church have the principle for investment that the other church has? If it does, then you can rest assured, revival is on the way. If not, however, it's time to roll up your sleeves and begin to find out what it is going to take to get the people talents in your church invested.

Money sitting in a jar somewhere has no hope for increase. Take that same money to the bank and put it in a simple savings account, and no matter how bad the rate of return, it will grow more than it did sitting in the jar. In retrospect, a member of a church who simply attends and supports the church (jar) is good to have, but if that same person were to become involved in the ministry of the church, to even a small degree, there is potential for growth where there was none before. Who are the people sitting on the pews in your church that you could begin to invest into ministry?

In the kingdom of God, God is always looking for increase, both in our personal ministries and in the church corporately. However, when the principle investment is in a downward or diminishing state, then the church is nowhere near in a position to have the kind of increase or growth that God would want to give.

Who are the pew-sitting principal investments in your church? They are those whom God has given you to bring into ministry. If Satan can cause those to fall away or become discouraged, then in effect, he is causing the principle that God has given you, to decrease. However, when you begin to invest those people that God has given you to work with, you are setting the church up for success (increase).

It's okay if your congregation doesn't have a 50% increase in one year. It's okay if it doesn't double next month. We all would like to have that kind of increase. We look at the book of Acts and the growth that took place there, and begin to measure ourselves by those people.

What we fail to realize, is that Jesus spent years reaching out to multiple thousands of people, without much immediate return. Any pastor in this world would want to have 3000 souls added to his church in one day. However, it is doubtful that there are many churches in this world who could handle that kind of growth. A church, especially those in ministry, must be taught and trained how to handle that kind of exponential growth.

Don't Minimize Small Successes

When we set out to position an individual for success in ministry, in essence we are positioning the whole church for success. Every small step an individual makes is a step of increase for the entire church body.

When we look at the parable of the talents, we notice that of the two men that increased their Lord's goods, one of them had twice the increase as the other. Yet their Master didn't condemn the one whose increase was only half as much.

Often we pay too much attention to the growth that other churches are having. It's very important to realize that the increase another church is having may be the result, not of the latest program their church is involved in, but rather the result of years of seed planting that has finally began to bear fruit.

When God gives a vision for ministry in the church, it is important to temper the vision with focusing on small successes and keeping momentum moving.

(Jim's thoughts)

When God speaks to me about my ministry or what He would have me to do for Him, He shows me the end from the beginning. The whole plan unfolds in my mind. I see each aspect come into place and how each one benefits and builds upon the other.

In the real world however, this vision is not so easily accomplished. People get in the way. Red tape slows it down. Financial limitations hinder it. Time constrains it.

If I became discouraged the first time someone said no, the vision God gave me die away. So, I have learned to let the plan unfold one piece at a time. It may not happen in the time I want it to. (It never does.) I want it done now, but I am finding that some of the things God has placed before me take years to accomplish. It may not happen with the people I thought God would use. It hardly ever happens the way I thought it would happen. Yet, it does happen. Why? Because God has created momentum so that nothing can stop it.

People may get in the way. Time constraints and money limitations may hinder it, but a true vision from Him will always come to fruition. Don't become disillusioned the first time things don't work out the way you want them to. Hang onto the vision. It's going to happen. If you keep the vision alive, you will see it happen. If you don't, another will pick it up and they will see it come to pass. Wouldn't you rather God use you?

When traveling, you often know you are going the right direction because occasionally you come across a sign on the side of the road that lets you know your destination is just ahead. These signs are sometimes very far apart. Oftentimes, you may question if you are going in the right direction because it has been a while since you last saw a sign pointing to your destination.

The same is true when it comes to the work of God. We often feel God direct us to a destination. He gives us a vision for it. So, we recruit those who will help us get the work of God to that destination. However, at some point in the journey, many become discouraged when they do not have a constant reminder in front of them that they are going in the right direction. At the first bump in the road, they pull over ready to give up. They think there should be no bumps in Vision road. However, Vision road is full of bumps. It is full of situations that would hinder or discourage someone who does not have a good hold on what God has called them to.

Watch for the signs. Focus on the small confirmations. You are not going to get to where you want to go overnight, so pay attention to the small successes. If it has been a while since you heard from God, keep doing the thing He told you to do the last time you heard from Him.

- The Bible says to despise not the day of small things. (Zech 4:10)
- Every victory, no matter how small, is still a victory.
- Every step forward, no matter what the size, is still a step in the right direction.

Keep building, line upon line, precept upon precept, here a little and there a little, you are gaining momentum. Keep it going! Don't give up!